SKIN AND CODE   Edited by Daniel Neugebauer, with contributions by Alyk Blue, Johanna Burai, Luce deLire, i-PÄD, Rhea Ramjohn, Calah P Toussaint-Amat, and Julia Velkova & Anne Kaun

Skin and Code

Edited by
Daniel Neugebauer

Contents

Skin and Code

Violence, both physical and metaphysical, leaves traces and creates reality. It is not difficult to imagine blue, green, or yellow bruises, the texture of bulging scars, the feeling of goosebumps or cracks in a crust of dry blood. It is easy to picture the consequences and causes of these skin changes: suffering or desire, trauma or death. While physical violence leaves traces on the skin, conceptual violence inscribes itself into interfaces via algorithms—as a pixelated prejudice, a memefied discrimination in secret chat groups. No healing without a second look at visible and invisible violence. Through heterogeneous languages and language uses, through vernaculars and styles, the assembled contributions attempt to trace the codes of violence, to circumscribe, expose, or comprehend them.

The coding and decoding of body surfaces and interfaces accompany everyday life and follow a variety of norms. These norms are not rigid, but a matrix of changing tastes, cultural influences, technical requirements, or physical possibilities. The horizons of thought and perception determine the nature of the codes and their legibility. The act of coding and decoding is a daily game of negotiating positions and affiliations. It is therefore important to ask which rules of play or conduct were created by whom and when. This game often becomes deadly serious for marginalized people and ideas.

If you scratch at skin, flesh emerges, if you scratch at codes, prejudices appear. Readers are invited to scratch at the surface of the book's pages.

The collected contributions create an interdisciplinary noise between surface structures and the occasional deepening. Luce deLire asks: Can Spinoza's intellectual cosmos help us to recognize the contradictions of a binary coded but heterogeneously structured digital reality? And what role did discrimination play in the development of Spinoza's world of thought? The visuals of Alyk Blue connect the Enlightenment era with the digital present. In a kind of lyrical semiotics Rhea Ramjohn pulls out all the stops to give sensual form to multiple identities, voices, and languages—but she also knows how to reflect healing: the texture of an avocado skin forms an interface between generations, local identities, and personal narratives. Social scientists Anne Kaun and Julia Velkova take us behind the façade of the Net's neutrality in their critical analysis of the digital tools and culprits that standardize our online existence, our search and viewing behavior. How can users undermine the rules of algorithms and collectively fix carcinogenic codes? With its guide to the DENIZ method, the Initiative for Intersectional Pedagogy (i-PÄD) in Berlin breaks new ground in teaching anti-discriminatory codes of seeing in learning spaces: How do you read a torso that raises more questions than it answers?

Using the tools of philosophy, pedagogy, poetry, and politics, contributors to this volume penetrate surfaces, skins, and interfaces layer by layer—measuring, changing, or healing them. Taken together, they lay down traces of words, which, as a form of counter-coding, help to leave zones of violence behind.

Daniel Neugebauer

Translated from the German by Kevin Kennedy

#MSOV
(modern surviving object / I / fied vernac)

I. Modernity in Vernacular

that inverted mountain of a molehill—that dip of her spine—a
natural place for the saddled thigh of her thumb to rest so easily upon.

why they don't do that here?
pressing palms on what they say is small.

watch all— my grandmother's bent wrist akimbo made to fit just so.
arms know just where to go.
is like,
to leave them there just swinging on the sides, is like leaving an
anchor in water—nah touching sand.
mornings she rest the left one there, right one scrubbing away at
teeth I thought was shell. and mommy still says stories—
dem old men using sugar cane to polish gums back then.

every place I've been seemed to speak languages that contradict
themselves.
sugar nah good for no mouth.
except, how shall I contradict elders who live longer than babes?
well, modernity is bold faced and big smile. and sometimes yuh
have to buy the Colgate with the car.
white paste turn to ritual with enamel cup instead of calabash.
But at least we had the cock to crow longside to know, we was not
like them.

morning air still and cool and like new baby smell? the sharp rays
of the sun triangulating punctuating a sky looking like that light pink
part of the melon rind. and the cock crowing on the right. some-
where on the spaced out sideways fingers a de zaboca.
Like he waiting years, like we, fuh that long bearing swelling avocado seed. Caribbean privilege is patience. knowing how to fix
yuh plate to de season.

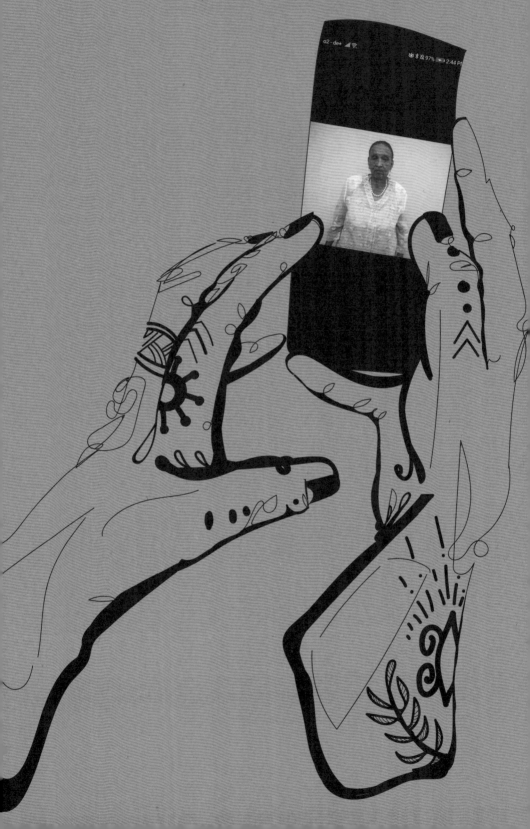

I forget to mention, brushing teeth happened in the inside outside.
Upon the veranda, and open to the heavens spitting Colgate mouth
water out onto the pitch. and I wondered, as the little child, well
why? we must walk upon the pitch, past morning spit, but grandma
treated the ground below like the place for throwing all kinds of
water, and Colgate could well have been Jergens, Palmolive, or
Squeezy. is only cheeks and biceps that did the flushing round there.
Now this grandma's little grandchild lived in a house with the
post code pampering of an address, a satellite dish, and a doorbell.
then somebody called me a millennial the other day,

"oh you millennials, you don't know how to do anything
without your phones."

there was a woman in my grandmother's village who had a landline.
when we called from them dark days in Massachusetts, my favorite
part was when she would say, *hol on*, and the 6 minute lapse of the
receiver, sitting on a doily no doubt, still picking up those muffled
steps as she went to fetch grandma. them birds, once in a while, them
birds would sing *tune boi tune*! or the t.v. sounds of my people's
voices ping—ponged picong in the background. 6 minutes of familiar
quiet— like it not going to ghost you.

so my cousin captured her and now she lives in my WhatsApp folder.
some JPEGs and few thousand pixels buzz around and vibrate to
make up this thing called my grandmother.
standing back to wall with her arms swinging on each side.
wah iz dis?
she look like she nah touching sand.

so this download is
8 miscarriages,
and butter on beaten back,
and rum punch breath,
with Parliament cut eye,
and colonial birth certificate and plantation upbringing
is my grandmother with the enamel Colgate cup?
I pass the WhatsApp pic round my cypher in Kreuzberg and
everybody loves a hero. a shero.

everybody love a strong man, especially when is a 'oman.
and tomorrow morning?
is them who will eat she avocado toast eh?

II. Surviving in Vernacular

go and wash yuh hand.

washing, and buckets, and toting, and collecting in blue plastic
drums agape, greedy for water.

fish with closed mouths don't get caught.

but water, water must be ketched, collected, constrained.
how gentle we balance that basin,
and those who are rough, they are the ones who take it all for granted.

"I was born for this"
I was reared for this.

*"Don't waste that water! Come give here. Use de ole
water to water dem plants."*

I saw a documentary on sustainable water cycle systems.
Turns out every mother of my mother and my mother was right.
At least I spent only the first 30 years hiding—recycling, collecting,
re-using.
The next 30 I can boast about being reared in sustainable waste
management systems.

The pandemic hit and I had 64 1-liter bottles in my basement.
Always prepping for disaster.

I am not who they are expecting to survive this.
But I know my blood, though I know not its names.
She and He and They lived and breathed and bled crossed oceans,
hunger, and whipping pain, cutting cane, rape and maim.
I survive the other-ing.

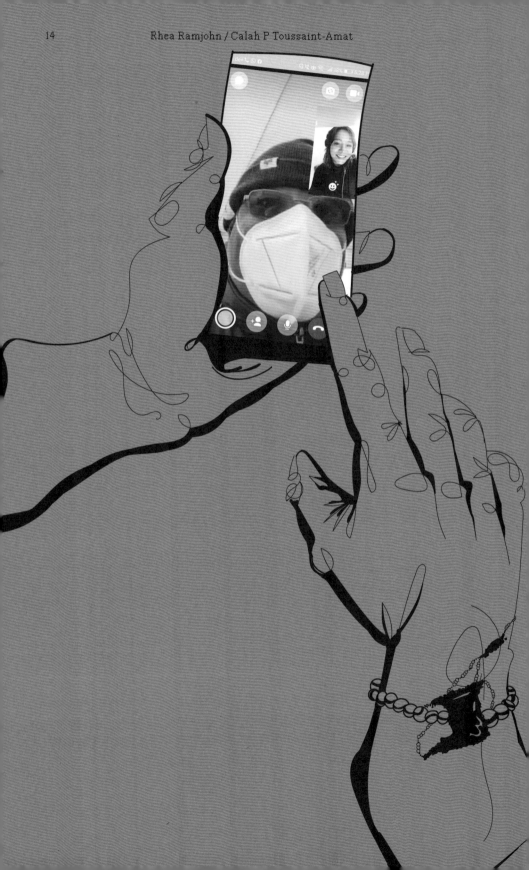

Now they tell us the keys to survival are masking and washing and
dis tan cing.

I turn my face to the point where the 2 walls meet in their thick concrete seams.
You could say I was standing in a corner.
My right thumb almost numb and most certainly cramped—
petrified into that hook form as it held down the WhatsApp green mic:

> *"Well, I'm doing ok, or I guess not, 'cause I been thinking....'*
> *cause yooo....there will be so many of us who die this year!"*

And I screamed—I howled the honest howl of a thousand deaths.
And the cops hadn't even killed Breonna Taylor yet.

> *"The numbers. The numbers. They don't realize—or maybe they just*
> *don't care—'cause we're the ones who have to go out to work—*
> *go out there. Oh my god yall—every nurse, every train driver,*
> *all the people working shift work—these are my people and we'll all be*
> *dead! Oh my god, we'll statistically be literally less black*
> *and brown people on the face of this planet by the end of this year!"*

The chant got louder,
Black Lives Matter!
and all the screens went black instead.
Social.   Media.   ███████████

I found time to call my mother.
Then my brother, who was the last one, at his lot, left.
He said,

> *Yuh have to give dem a 'how you holdin' up today man?' or a 'hang in*
> *there buddy' so they doh feel like you a threat yuh know? Cuse*
> *dey cyah see half meh face now, with de mask, so yuh know, they doh*
> *know I iz no threat—yuh know wah I mean?*

yes, I know what he means. We all put on that mask long before we
dipped a toe on that shore:
Reduce accent—check

Neutralize opinion—check
Be the bootstrapped token—check
System optimized.
Waste management design.

Waste not want not.

III. Object / I / fied in Vernac

In Cambridge, my blue-veined friend took me to a second-hand shop,
        You can find the BEST shit here.
Browsing the stuffed racks, I didn't let on that my adolescence was an
entire hand-me-down.
The faux-fur lined coat the truthful octogenarian gave me at eighteen.
I wasn't cold. Just brown like take-away bag and ... optimistically
unprepared.

This writer asked me once,
        What's wrong with the word exotic?

🔊 **exotic**
/ɪɡˈzɒtɪk,ɛɡˈzɒtɪk/

See definitions in:

All   Physics   Chemistry   Plant

adjective

    originating in or characteristic of a distant foreign country.
    "exotic birds"

    Similar: foreign   non-native   tropical   alien   imported   introduced
    unnaturalized   faraway   far off   far-flung   unfamiliar   distant   remote
    Opposite: native   familiar   nearby   ⌃

noun

    an exotic plant or animal.
    "he planted exotics in the sheltered garden"

Far flung felt correct. not spillt like dribble from a careless basin.
Thrown water onto the pitch. but thrown with momentum.
like ole water inna de bush
or paper bag inna de trash

like ole coat inna de pile for re-sale mother's chile.

None of us are entitled.
So many of us take.

I take more and long and deep breaths
reclaiming my time like Representative Waters
and pushing through the tide.
I breathe underwater.
I take.
and take them more.
take for Mr. Garner and take for Mr. Floyd.
take meh own breath because it is barely given.
take without permission
take because promise is comforter a fool.

it has become apparent,
allyuh take meh
good nature for free labor

when ah tell yuh,
no behaviour!
steuuuuuuuuuuuuuups
wait dere an tink I is goat shit waiting on hill.

chile, I iz de wind.
Iz me who go bus yuh belly an make rain fall.
YOU—who is always imposing like storm,
expectin i go forgive all allyuh wrongs?
naaaah boi nah!
steuuuuuuuuuuuuuuuuups
meh eye big and meh memory fast

wait dere an tink I is goat shit waiting on hill.
when all meh good nature gone,
where yuh free labor coming from?

it has become apparent

allyuh take meh good nature an ...

well is no behaviour yuh dun leave behind,
so doh watch me so when i give you de cut-eye-
is split I go split dat belly dou-dou,
and collect meh rain-water
in every measure of timely manner.
wait dere an tink I iz yuh free labor!
iz YOU sitting on hill, but like cow shit,
waiting for wind to blow.

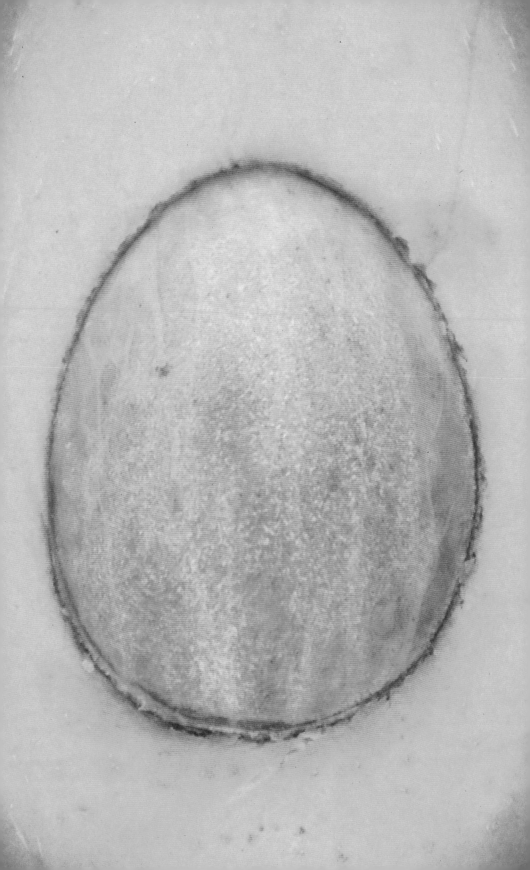

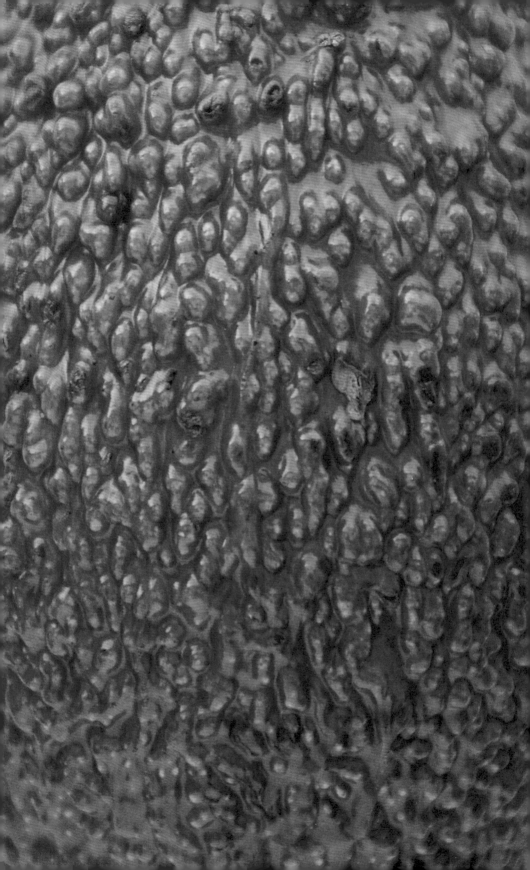

"[E]very day the matter seems to get worse, and I don't know what I should do."[1]

Violence, Spinozism, and Digital Reality

The Violence of Philosophy

Concepts are like commodities: Once they enter the theoretical vernacular, a.k.a. the intellectual marketplace of ideas, they shed their bloody skin. Nothing shall testify of their brutal process of production. A materialism about knowledge must therefore be a philosophy of violence—a reflection of and about the violence, constitutive of the philosophical enterprise in general. In the words of Patrice Douglas and Frank Wilderson: "We need to imagine metaphysical violence rather than a metaphysics that violence destroys."[2]

One example for this violent production is what Gayatri Chakravorty Spivak calls "sanctioned ignorance."[3] Sara Ahmed puts it as follows:

> Once on twitter I pointed out that an author had mainly cited other white men. He agreed with my description of the pattern but said that the pattern 'was in the traditions that had influenced him.' To be influenced by a tradition is to be citing white men. Citing; reciting; an endless retrospective. White men as a well-trodden path; the more we tread *that way* the more we go *that way*. To move forward you follow the traces left behind of those who came before. But in following these traces, in participating in their becoming brighter, becoming lighter, other traces fade out, becoming shadows, places unlit; eventually they disappear. Women too, people of colour too, might cite white men: to be you have to be in relation to white men (to

---

1 Baruch Spinoza, Ep. 68. As to the referencing of Spinoza's works, please see the note on page 48.

2 Patrice Douglas and Frank Wilderson, "The Violence of Presence: Metaphysics in a Blackened World," *The Black Scholar*, vol. 43, no. 4 (Winter 2013), pp. 117–23, here p. 122.

3 Gayatri Chakravorty Spivak, *A Critique of Postcolonial Reason.* Cambridge, MA: Harvard University Press, 1999; p. 3.

twist a Fanonian point). Not to cite white men is not to exist;
or at least not to exist within this or that field. When you exercise
these logics, you might come to exist, by writing out another
history, another way of explaining your existence. If to cite is to
wipe out your history, what then?[4]

In any case, "[you] must be prepared for the worst [says Spivak]:
appropriation or hostility based on the sanctioned ignorance of both
elite theorist and self-styled activist, in different spheres."[5]

Sometimes, in conversation, the omitted violence of conceptual
production makes itself felt. People shrink back, deny interaction,
opt out of what they perceive as submission to an external authority that wants to crush their thoughts and submit their will. Some of
them locate this felt resistance to the process of thinking itself and go
the way of emotional exploration instead.[6] They take all knowledge
that is being articulated within a certain tradition as an instrument
of violence of this tradition—the white, Western, colonial, hetero-
cis-patriarchal tradition, that is. A counter-knowledge is articulated
in and through this resistance, a knowledge of the omitted violence
done in order to reach a conceptual clarity, which presents itself as
seamless persuasion, with no strings attached.

But on crucial points, the white, cis-hetero-patriarchal tradition
is not identical with itself. In a crucial way, the history of Western
Enlightenment is such a case and Spinoza is key to understanding this.

In the following pages, I will exemplify metaphysical violence
in two ways: For one, I will demonstrate how metaphysical violence
shapes the European Enlightenment in the case of Spinoza. Secondly,
I will unearth an omitted dimension of his philosophy, namely *conceptual distinctions* as distinctions that are neither *real* nor *accidental/*

---

4   Sara Ahmed, "White Men," *feministkilljoys.com* (posted 2014), https:
     //feministkilljoys.com/2014/11/04/white-men/, accessed October 20,
     2020.
5   Spivak, *A Critique of Postcolonial Reason*, p.86.
6   This, I take it, is a contemporary version of an esoteric tradition. See also
     Luce deLire, "The New Queer," Public Seminar (posted 2019), https:
     //publicseminar.org/essays/the-new-queer/, accessed October 22,
     2020; and Luce deLire, "Queer Feminist Witchcraft," in Katharina Rein
     (ed.), *Magic. Genre Fiction and Film Companions*. Bern: Peter Lang,
     forthcoming 2021.

modal. Lastly, I will apply the theory of *conceptual distinctions* to a principal mode of contemporary *corpoliteracy*: the Internet.

The Legacy

The European Enlightenment, at least partially, was built as explicit repression and distorting appropriation of a particular philosopher—Spinoza. Spinoza was not a figure on the sidelines of the Enlightenment—and, thus, the creation of *whiteness*, the nation state, and the civilizing mission—but front and center as its principal enemy, its most beloved Atheist—partially because of his radical views and partially because of his Jewish identity.

"Spinoza is one of the most important philosophers—and certainly the most radical—of the early modern period."[7] However, "[t] o my knowledge, no philosopher has been simultaneously embraced and rejected for as many reasons as has Spinoza."[8] In fact, Spinoza has more than once been embraced by and through rejection and inversely been rejected by way of embrace. Regarding the Western philosophical tradition, this is no small matter. In fact, Spinoza and Spinozism[9] became the engine of the efforts of a European Enlightenment on all sides and a unifying force for both the Counter-Enlightenment as well as a moderate Enlightenment,[10] which could present themselves palatable to the reigning powers of the European seventeenth and eighteenth centuries exactly by distancing themselves from Spinoza.
"But why was there such a vehement reaction against Spinoza?"[11] The reason is twofold: For one, "Spinoza represented the extreme left

7 Steven Nadler, "Baruch Spinoza," in Edward N. Zalta (ed.), *The Stanford Encyclopedia of Philosophy* (Summer 2020), https://plato.stanford.edu /archives/sum2020/entries/spinoza/.

8 Idit Dobbs-Weinstein, *Spinoza's Critique of Religion and its Heirs: Marx, Benjamin, Adorno.* Cambridge: Cambridge University Press, 2015, p. 21.

9 "Admittedly, what was called 'Spinozism' *was* often far sketchier and cruder than Spinoza himself." See Jonathan Israel, *Enlightenment Contested: Enlightenment, Modernity, and the Emancipation of Man* 1670-1752. Oxford: Oxford University Press, 2008, p. 47.

10 Jonathan Israel, *Radical Enlightenment: Philosophy and the Making of Modernity.* Oxford: Oxford University Press, 2002, p. 22.

11 Frederick C. Beiser, *The Fate of Reason: German Philosophy from Kant to Fichte.* Cambridge, MA: Harvard University Press, 1987, pp. 49-50.

wing in seventeenth- and eighteenth-century religious and political conviction."[12] In fact, "all Early Enlightenment thinkers, major and minor, that is many dozens of writers, took it for granted that Spinoza was the pre-eminent 'Atheist' of the era."[13] Spinoza had earned this reputation not just by way of his excommunication from the Jewish community in Amsterdam in 1656, but also with his authorship of the *Theologico-Political Treatise*,[14] (TTP, "a book forged in hell")[15] in 1670. The TTP argues, among other things that the Old and the New Testament may be explained entirely by scientific means and are of ethical and political value at best, that miracles do not exist, and that freedom of thought and speech should be the basis of every flourishing political community.

Just after his early death at the age of forty-four (February 1677) in the Netherlands, Spinoza's friends mobilized to edit and publish the works he left behind, entailing the famous *Ethics*, where Spinoza lays out his metaphysics and a full ethical as well as political program, based on a scientific theory of human affects. The project succeeded in early 1678 but the book was quickly prohibited by Dutch authorities—a practice which was to be followed by many other European powers. "[This] edict [...] had an appreciable significance in shaping attitudes and fixing the status of ideas, laying down legally the separation between radical and moderate Enlightenment which, within a few years, was to extend across the whole of Europe."[16]

Yet why were people so eager to identify Spinoza with atheism in particular? "Of course, part of the answer lies in Spinoza's Jewish ancestry."[17] In fact, "Spinoza's detractors could draw on fifteen hundred years of research attributing Jewish origins to skepticism, materialism and atheism."[18] Consequentially, famous figures such as

12   Ibid.
13   Israel, *Enlightenment Contested*, p. 45.
14   Baruch Spinoza, "Theologico-Political Treatise," in Curley (ed.), *The Collected Works of Spinoza, Volume 2*.
15   Quoted from a malevolent pamphlet of anonymous authorship in: Jacob Freudenthal, *Spinoza - Sein Leben und seine Lehre - Erster Band: Das Leben Spinozas*. Stuttgart: Frohmanns Verlag 1904, p. 131. See ibid. for details regarding the probable authors.
16   Israel, *Radical Enlightenment*, p. 294.
17   Beiser, *The Fate of Reason*, p. 49.
18   David Nirenberg, *Anti-Judaism: The History of a Way of Thinking*. New York: W. W. Norton & Company, 2014, e-book, n. p.

the philosopher Henry More and Pierre Bayle (whose *Historical and Critical Dictionary* (1697) was a catalyst for the European Enlightenment at large) drew the line from Jew through Cartesian to Atheist without batting an eye. And a "new wave of research into Judaism was motivated, at least in part, by the widespread conviction that the new atheistic philosophies were descendants of Judaism, and that the war against them needed to target the source."[19]

Simultaneously, however, it became possible to portray Spinoza as the "good Jew," who, by way of overcoming his heritage, played well into the Christian idea of Judaism as something to be superseded and eventually destroyed. Spinoza gives some reason for this reading by his tendentially negative depiction of Jews in the TTP. "[H]is deployment of the Jews may have been part of a rhetorical strategy to persuade his audience by drawing on its prejudices."[20] Or else it might have originated in Spinoza's particular experience in Amsterdam at the time.[21] However, it was easy enough for Spinoza's contemporaries to use him as a poster child of anti-Jewish sentiment *exactly because he was a Jew.*

In this function as the non-Jewish Jew, Spinoza was baptized during the so-called *Pantheismusstreit* (Pantheism debate) in Germany in the 1780s.[22] Friedrich Heinrich Jacobi, a dedicated Catholic

19   Ibid.
20   Ibid.
21   Yitzhak Melamed, "Spinoza and the Election of the Hebrews," in Michael A. Rosenthal (ed.), *Spinoza & Modern Jewish Philosophy*. London: Palgrave Macmillan, forthcoming.
22   For more on the history of Spinoza's reception and Spinozism in the Enlightenment, see Israel, *Radical Enlightenment*; and Israel, *Enlightenment Contested*. For the history of Spinozism in Germany in particular, see Ursula Goldenbaum, "The Pantheismusstreit—Milestone or Stumbling Block in the German Reception of Spinoza?," in Michael Hampe, Ursula Renz, and Robert Schnepf (eds), *Spinoza's Ethics: A Collective Commentary*. Leiden: Brill, 2011, pp. 325–51; and Ursula Goldenbaum, "Spinoza – Ein toter Hund? Nicht für Christian Wolff," *Zeitschrift für Ideengeschichte*, vol. 5, no. 1 (Spring 2011), pp. 29–41. And for an analysis of Spinozism in the Soviet Union and the GDR, see Klaus-Dieter Eichler, "Travestie und Ideologie. Spinoza bei Marx und im Denken der DDR," *Zeitschrift für Ideengeschichte*, vol. 5, no. 1 (Spring 2011), pp. 42–60. For a recent analysis of the role of Spinoza in twenty-first-century Post-Marxist philosophy see Katja Diefenbach, *Spekulativer Materialismus. Spinoza in der Postmarxistischen Philosophie*. Vienna: Transcript, 2018.

and philosopher of the Counter-Enlightenment, had initiated the complex debate in order to discredit the then-most famous living German philosopher, Moses Mendelssohn.[23] The latter, however, had claimed the possibility of a Jewish Enlightenment—the *Has-kalah*—in a book entitled *Jerusalem or About Spiritual Power and Jewishness* (1783), which greatly angered those who believed that Enlightenment was to be had only under the condition of the Christian faith, meaning: the German Enlightenment mainstream. In a surprising turn of events, Jacobi's anti-Jewish strategy worked out beyond expectation: The more Spinoza became palatable to the German mainstream, "the more Mendelssohn became, for the Christian audience, again simply the Jewish, and the despised philosopher."[24] Spinoza—the Jew, the Cartesian, the Atheist—had become not only a Christian but also a weapon against Jewish Emancipation in the service of the Counter-Enlightenment. He was then transformed into a bootstrap for the rise of Kantianism: For the Pantheism debate had framed the following alternative: Either, so Jacobi, the project of philosophical rationalism gave way to a resurgence of Christian piety, or else "all rationalism would finally lead to Spinozism [and thus Atheism], [which] made people think about an alternative and so Kant was suddenly a focus of attention, even though his *Critique* had hardly been read previously."[25] In a way, then, the Christianization of Spinoza as an instrument of the dismissal of Jewish Emancipation was the ground on which Immanuel Kant and German idealism would flourish.[26]

The European Enlightenment, then, is not just a product of violence against *all other knowledge*. Rather, it does have a primary declared enemy, who later on is being introjected: Spinoza. Spinoza, therefore, is a paradigmatic case for the study of metaphysical violence

23   Goldenbaum, "*The Pantheismusstreit*," p. 340.
24   Ibid., pp. 340–41.
25   Ibid., p. 346.
26   On Kant's own anti-Semitism, see Dobbs-Weinstein, *Spinoza's Critique of Religion*, p. 41. See also J. Kameron Carter, *Race: A Theological Account*. New York: Oxford University Press, 2008, pp. 79–125. This, however, is not the end of the story. Fast forward: "[T]he repeated condemnations have [today] been replaced by a celebration of [Spinoza's] secular heresy [as a result of his Christianization] by philosophers of radically different ilk [such as Steven Smith and Toni Negri]." (Dobbs-Weinstein, *Spinoza's Critique of Religion*, p. 22).

(as outlined above).[27] Once we look at it from this perspective, this violence is tangible everywhere. For example in the following question:

Was Spinoza White?

The short answer: It is unclear. That alone should give us pause. In pre-nineteenth-century Europe, it was taken largely for granted that, "Jews look different, they have a different appearance, [...]. Skin color marked the Jew as both different and diseased."[28] We may take the following quote from François-Maximilien Misson, originally published in 1691 (fourteen years after Spinoza's death), as an example:

> It is [...] [an] error to say that all Jews were browned [*basannez*]: that is not true, except for the Jews of Portuguese race [*race Portugaise*—such as Spinoza]. Those people always marry among each other and the children resemble their fathers and mothers, and their brown/dark [*brun*] complexion is thus perpetuated without much diminuition, wherever they live, even in the Northern regions. But the Jews who are originally German, such as for example those in Prague, do not have a darker complexion [*n'ont pas le teint plus basané*] than any of their countrymen.[29]

27   For Spinoza's implications into the colonial endeavors of his time, see Diefenbach, *Spekulativer Materialismus*, p. 221.

28   Sander L. Gilman, "Are Jews White? Or, the History of the Nose Job," in Les Back and John Solomos (eds), *Theories of Race and Racism: A Reader*. London: Routledge, 2000, pp. 229–37, here p. 233. On the racialization of Jews, see Christina von Braun, "Und der Feind ist Fleisch geworden. Der rassistische Antisemitismus," in Christina von Braun and Ludger Heid (eds), *Der Ewige Judenhass*. Berlin: Philo Verlagsgesellschaft, 2000, pp. 149–213, here p. 156; and Nirenberg, *Anti-Judaism*. On the relations between anti-Black racism and anti-Semitism, see Carter, *Race: A Theological Account*, p. 120.

29   François-Maximilien Misson, *Nouveau voyage d'Italie: avec un mémoire contenant des avis utiles à ceux qui voudront faire le mesme voyage* (4th ed.), vol. 2., La Haye: Henri van Bulderen 1702, p. 126. However, "this was a minority position" (see Gilman, "Are Jews White?," p. 231). Curiously, the 1714 English translation has 'black' for 'basannez.' See François-Maximilien Misson, *A New Voyage to Italy*, vol. 2. London: R. Bonwicke, 1714, p. 139. Many thanks to Till Bardoux for pressing me on this issue.

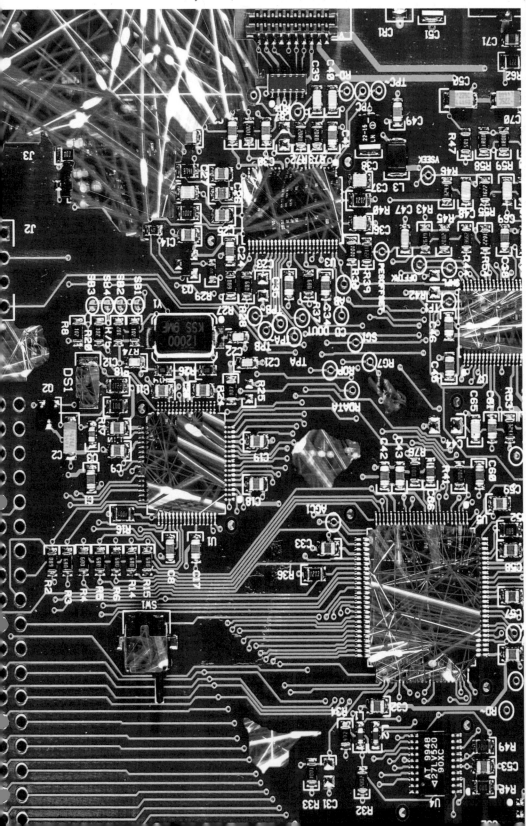

Now, even if ethnic and racist discourses might not yet have been in full gear by the later seventeenth century in the Netherlands regarding Jews,[30] we may still think that when Georg Wilhelm Friedrich Hegel describes the single known visual depiction of Spinoza in a painting of unknown providence as "mild and benevolent" in his lectures on the history of philosophy (delivered on a regular basis between 1805 and 1831),[31] the tide has turned. For in the nineteenth century, Orientalism is the order of the day.[32] In fact, "[O]rientalism and modem anti-Semitism have common roots,"[33] says Edward Said. "The Jews and the Muslims, as subjects of Orientalist study, were readily understandable in view of their primitive origins: this was (and to a certain extent still is) the cornerstone of modern Orientalism."[34] In exactly this sense, Hegel sees in Spinoza's philosophy "an echo from Eastern lands. The Oriental view of absolute identity was brought by Spinoza much closer to (or even introduced into) the European way of thinking, and more specifically the European and Cartesian philosophy."[35] To Hegel, Spinoza, in fact, is (as Said says) "readily understandable in view of [his] primitive origins," namely (as Hegel has it) "very simple,

30   For more on this see Marla Brettschneider, *The Family Flamboyant: Race Politics, Queer Families, Jewish Lives*. Albany, NY: State University of New York Press, 2012, p. 25; and Matthew Frye Jacobson, "Looking Jewish, Seeing Jews," in Matthew Frye Jacobson, *Whiteness of a Different Color: European Immigrants and the Alchemy of Race*. Cambridge, MA: Harvard University Press, 1999, pp. 171-99.

31   Georg Wilhelm Friedrich Hegel, *Vorlesungen über die Geschichte der Philosophie* III. Frankfurt am Main: Suhrkamp, 1971, p. 161.

32   For an extensive study of the role of Orientalism in the construction of the historiography of philosophy, see Catherine König-Prahong, *La Colonie Philosophique. Écrire L'histoire de la philosophie aux* XVIIIe-XIXe *Siècle*. Paris: EHESS, 2019.

33   Edward Said, *Orientalism*. New York: Vintage Books, 1979, p. xxiv.

34   Ibid., p. 234.

35   "[…] ein Nachklang des Morgenlandes. Die morgenländische Anschauung der absoluten Identität ist der europäischen Denkweise und näher dem europäischen, Cartesianischen Philosophieren unmittelbar nähergebracht, darein eingeführt worden." Hegel, *Geschichte* III, 1971, p. 158. The translation into "echo from Eastern lands" is from Georg Wilhelm Friedrich Hegel, *Lectures on the History of Philosophy*, trans. Elizabeth S. Haldane and Frances H. Simson, 3 vols. London: University of Nebraska Press, 1995, p. 252.

and on the whole easy to comprehend,"[36] despite some difficulties
that must be ascribed to a lack of skill on the side of its author. The
"echo from Eastern lands" curiously resides outside history:[37] It is
"the main standpoint, which *still* counts for Orientals—that of substance, the one substance. This pantheism, or Spinozism, if you like to
call it so, is thus the standpoint, the universal view of Oriental poets,
historians and philosophers."[38] In this last passage, which concerns
the philosophy of the medieval *Mu'tazilites* under the heading "Arabic Philosophy," Hegel projects an image of Spinoza back into history.
Said explains: "The Orient existed as a place isolated from the mainstream of European progress in the sciences, arts, and commerce."[39]
And so does Spinoza, the Jew, the Oriental. To Hegel, Spinoza is nothing but his primitive origin—the "standpoint, the universal view of
Oriental[s]"—systematically articulated and, therefore, palatable
to the occidental mind. Spinoza's philosophy captures an ahistorical
proto-philosophy in a systematic form and thus enables the history
of philosophy while itself belonging to it only half way. In this sense,
Hegel proclaims, "either Spinozism or no philosophy at all."[40]
"By the latter half of the nineteenth century, Western European Jews
had become indistinguishable from other Western Europeans in mat-
ters of language, dress, occupation, location of their dwellings and the
cut of their hair."[41] Spinoza, however, seems to meander between var-

36   "Was sein System anbetrifft, so ist es sehr einfach und im ganzen leicht
     zu fassen." Hegel, *Geschichte III*, p. 161. Hegel is nevertheless full of
     praise for Spinoza, See Yitzhak Melamed, "Hegel, Spinoza, and McTaggart
     on the Reality of Time," in Dina Emundts and Sally Sedgwick (eds),
     International Yearbook of German Idealism, vol. 14 (2016), pp. 211-34,
     here p. 212-17.
37   Georg Wilhelm Friedrich Hegel, *Vorlesungen über die Geschichte der
     Philosophie I*. Frankfurt am Main: Suhrkamp, 1971, p. 121.
38   "Sie haben so bei höherer Gedankenbildung den Hauptstandpunkt, der
     es noch für die Orientalen ist, die Substanz, die eine Substanz zum
     Bewußtsein gebracht. Dieser Pantheismus, wenn man will Spinozismus,
     ist so der Standpunkt, die allgemeine Ansicht der orientalischen Dichter,
     Geschichtsschreiber und Philosophen." (Georg Wilhelm Friedrich
     Hegel, *Vorlesungen über die Geschichte der Philosophie II*. Frankfurt am
     Main: Suhrkamp, 1971, p. 519).
39   Said, *Orientalism*, p. 206.
40   "Entweder Spinozismus oder keine Philosophie." (Hegel, *Geschichte I*,
     pp. 163-64).
41   Gilman, "Are Jews White?," p. 233.

touching

ious social positions—the Jew, the Atheist, the Christian, the Oriental, the first modern secularist. And in the following two twentieth-century descriptions of that same painting mentioned earlier, racialization still remains and retroactively echoes throughout the text:

> [T]he dark hair; the high, arched brows; the long, slightly hooked nose; the full lips; the high cheek-bones and the sallow or olive complexion.[42]

> His small eyes were dark and lively, his long eye-brows black like the curly hair that fell around his shoulders; his whole personality was captivating and everything, not least his brownish tint, betrayed his Portuguese-Jewish descent.[43]

Spinoza may not have been *not* white. But was he *white*? And since when? The exposition of this question must suffice as an answer for the moment. What we can see, however, is that Spinoza, the person and his philosophy have always been subject to violent appropriation, to a distorting integration into history as well as into systematic edifices. But the violence does not stop here. It lives in the heart of Spinoza's project and is constitutive of it.

The Language

Spinoza was a man of care and had to live and write most carefully. He used coded language and disguise in order to protect himself and enable publication of his writings. In this way, the violence of philosophical production can be found *within* Spinoza's text, trying to dodge the bullets of his opponents before they reach him. Spinoza's philosophy is a protective device as much as a full-on attack. Both are in fact indistinguishable.

For naturally, Spinoza knew of the dangerous climate he was moving in. In 1671, he urges his publisher not to translate the Latin TTP

---

42   Peter de Mendelssohn, "Did Spinoza Ever Sit for Rembrandt?," *Encounter*, vol. 49, no. 3 (1977), pp. 57–62, here p. 62.

43   Meinsma, quoted in Julien Levy, "Unknown Portrait of Spinoza," *The Connoisseur*, 1932, n. p; the original is in Koenrad Oege Meinsma, *Spinoza En Zijn Kring*. The Haag: Zuid Hollandsche Boek- en Handelsdrukkerij, 1896.

into Dutch, as he was worried that this would yield its prohibition.[44] In another letter, he advises his friend and interlocutor Ehrenfried Walther von Tschirnhaus to vet the young Gottfried Wilhelm Leibniz some more before "entrust[ing] [Spinoza's] writings to him."[45] And in 1675, he defers the publication of his magnum opus—*The Ethics* —because a rumor spread in Amsterdam, claiming "that a certain book [...] about God was in the press, and that in it [Spinoza] tried to show that there is no God."[46] "[E]very day the matter seems to get worse, and I don't know what I should do."[47] It is thus no wonder that in a letter from June 1676, Tschirnhaus acknowledges that some obfuscation might be necessary in their correspondence.[48] And in a note to the TTP that was published only after his death, Spinoza explicitly states that "the oppressiveness of our times does not permit me to explain"[49] certain things.

Nevertheless, in an act akin to victim blaming, language has been a touchstone of critique against Spinoza from early on. Spinoza and his followers were criticized for their "[v]eiled Expressions [and] coded language."[50] This is certainly true—however Spinoza had good reasons for this within the political climate of the time. However, "according to Leibniz, part of the clarity of language resides in its common usage and therefore linguistic innovation in philosophy always produces obscurity. Excessive innovation is a vice," and Spinoza its primary perpetrator.[51] To Leibniz, then, Spinoza's protective gear against violence and prohibition becomes itself a reason for his dismissal. And this tradition, this argument for the clarity of language, lives on up to the present day.

TL;DR: The violence of philosophical production is inscribed into the way in which Spinoza's metaphysics is produced. The latter, while envisioning the destruction of certain dogmas, is itself deeply

---

44   Spinoza, Ep. 44
45   Spinoza, Ep. 72.
46   Spinoza, Ep. 68.
47   Ibid.
48   Spinoza, Ep. 82.
49   Spinoza, TTP, 10.1, ADN 21, III/14.
50   Israel, *Radical Enlightenment*, p. 309.
51   Mogens Laerke, "The Problem of Alloglossia. Leibniz on Spinoza's Innovative Use of Philosophical Language," *British Journal for the History of Philosophy*, vol. 17, no. 5 (2009), pp. 939–53, here p. 940.

shaped by the violent conditions it grew out of. In turn, the rejection of Spinoza's philosophy is partially justified exactly with reference to that protective gear. It is *because* Spinoza's philosophy is hard to read that some people—such as Leibniz—reject it. Yet it is hard to read partially *because* Spinoza knew that people would reject his thoughts and that this rejection might be dangerous to him and his followers. In that way, then, those enjoying a more solid social standing turn Spinoza's precarious political position against him. Thus, violence begets violence.

The Heterogeneity of Reality

However, yet again, metaphysical violence does not stop here. It stretches further, right into the conceptual foundations of Spinoza's philosophy. A central element of Spinoza's philosophy is his theory of distinctions. *Something* is going on with Spinoza's theory of distinctions.[52] But the scarcity of his commentary on the issue makes it very elusive. The crucial twist is his rearticulation of the Cartesian "conceptual distinction."[53] In Spinoza's version, things are *conceptually distinct* if they are *really* (and necessarily) differentiated in the intellect (but not *produced by* the intellect), but not in the thing itself. I will elaborate on this shortly. Spinoza never details his theory of distinctions. In fact, he barely talks about it. Arguably, an otherwise omitted Judeo-Arabic philosophical materialism is rearticulated and modernized here. This tradition had been suppressed in the Christian West at least since the edict of 1277, which prohibited the philosophy of Muhammad ibn Rushd (or Averroes, a principal philosopher of the Islamic Arabic tradition) and violently enacted that prohibition.[54]

52   Deleuze recognizes this correctly, but inscribes Spinoza into a Christian tradition by way of linking him to Scotistic "formal distinctions." See Gilles Deleuze, *Expressionism in Philosophy: Spinoza.* New York: Zone Books, 1992 [1968], p. 27. For a critique of such reinscription, see Dobbs-Weinstein, *Spinoza's Critique of Religion.* Martial Gueroult agrees about this importance, but takes another route: see Martial Gueroult, *Spinoza I - Dieu.* Hildesheim: Georg Olms Verlagsbuchhandlung, 1969, p. 155.

53   Yitzhak Melamed, "The Building Blocks of Spinoza's Metaphysics: Substance, Attributes, and Modes," in Michael Della Rocca (ed.), *The Oxford Handbook of Spinoza.* New York: Oxford University Press, 2018.

54   See for example: Jan A. Aertsen, Kent Emery, Jr., and Andreas Speer (eds), *After the Condemnation of 1277. Philosophy and Theology at the University of Paris in the Last Quarter of the Thirteenth Century: Studies

The medieval Jewish and Islamic traditions of Aristotelianism, mostly written in Arabic, according to Idit Dobbs-Weinstein, had a tendency to favor "fluid, aspectival relation[s]," [55] especially regarding percep-

and Texts. Berlin: De Gruyter, 2011; J. M. M. H. Thijssen, *Censure and Heresy at the University of Paris*, 1200-1400. Philadelphia, PA: University of Pennsylvania Press, 1998; Alexander S. Jensen, "The Unintended Consequences of the Condemnation of 1277: Divine Power and the Established Order in Question," *Colloquium*, vol. 41, no. 1 (May 2009), pp. 57-72; Luca Bianchi, "New Perspectives on the Condemnation of 1277 and its Aftermath," *Recherches de théologie et philosophie médiévales*, vol. 70, no. 1 (2003), pp. 206-29; and classically, Pierre Duhem, *Le Système du Monde; Histoire des Doctrines Cosmologiques de Platon à Copernic*. Paris: Hermann, 1954.

55   "Of all the aspects of modern philosophy, the one that is literally unintelligible from the perspective of the pre-Modern materialist tradition, but also the one that is foundational to Modern philosophy, is the unified, isolated, or independent subject. For, in the absence of dualism, there can be no determined, unified subject independent of sensible 'objects'; rather there is a fluid, aspectival relation between affection and action, the sense, sensation, and sensed, whereby the more an individual is affected, the more she comes to be in act and in turn can affect others in the same respect. What can be said to be unified is experience (*empereia*), which comes about by repeated sensations, where sensation is the result of the aspectival relation between the sensing and the sensed. *Empereia* is indeed material, but it is certainly not immediate, let alone transparent to a sensing subject. This is one of the most significant dimensions of the materialist tradition that not only becomes literally unintelligible with the emergence of the modern subject but also that is suppressed and repressed. It is in virtue of this repression that John Locke, *inter alii*, can claim to follow Aristotle and is counted as an Aristotelian." (Dobbs-Weinstein, *Spinoza's Critique of Religion*, p. 35). According to Dobbs-Weinstein (ibid., pp. 36-39), the basic features of (Christian) modernity, resulting from the (dualistic) unity of the isolated subject are

1.   The need for certainty.
2.   The formation of the individual self.
3.   The anchoring of conceptual certainty in the individual self (such as certainty as absence of doubt in the mind for Descartes, surrender of individual power for the collective good in Hobbes, etc.).
4.   Split of recurrent time from teleological time, resulting in a divide of mechanic necessity (which recurs through efficient causes) from teleological necessity (which is purpose-driven by final causes).
5.   Separation of theory and practice and reinvention of practice as application of knowledge. Politics and ethics become instrumental application of preordained theories rather than lived practice.

tion and the generation of knowledge, over unified, isolated, and independent things (you, me, the transatlantic slave trade, etc., etc.), which dominate Christian philosophies to the present day.[56] These latter distinctions, into numerically differentiated, allegedly independent, and in any case isolated unities (sunflowers, bathrooms, ideas, violent conditions), are commonly called *real distinctions*. According to Spinoza, however, there are *no* real distinctions.[57] In fact, everything is integrated into absolutely infinite reality,[58] a.k.a. God or Nature.[59]

In this picture (or my understanding of it), things are radically different from themselves and achieve unity only in relation to other things. Speaking with Namita Goswami, things are fundamentally *heterogeneous*.[60] That does *not* mean that we have different perspectives on any one reality that remains essentially removed (that would be the Kantian idea). Rather, we are asked to grasp reality in itself as

6.   Formation of the nation state as the myth of individual surrender for the higher good of the collective.

7.   Justification of the submission or conquering of body/nature/Jew for the sake of salvation (as an instance of teleological necessity).

56   On the relation between Spinoza and Ibn Rushd, see Carlos Fraenkel, "Spinoza on Philosophy and Religion: The Averroistic Sources," in Carlos Fraenkel, Dario Perinetti, and Justin H. E. Smith (eds), *The Rationalists: Between Tradition and Innovation*. Berlin: Springer, 2011; and Bilal Elbazi, "The Concepts of Causality and Determinism: Between Averroes and Baruch Spinoza," *Tabayyun*, vol. 8. no. 32 (April 2020), pp. 31–58 (Arabic). Also interesting in this regard is Ernst Bloch, *Avicenna and the Aristotelian Left*. New York: Columbia University Press, 2019 [1963]. On Spinoza and Judeo-Arabic philosophy, see Zev Harvey Warren, "Portrait of Spinoza as a Maimonidean," *Journal of the History of Philosophy*, vol. 19, no. 2 (1981), pp. 151–72; and Yitzhak Melamed, "Hasdai Crescas and Spinoza on Actual Infinity and the Infinity of God's Attributes," in Steven Nadler (ed.), *Spinoza and Jewish Philosophy*. Cambridge: Cambridge University Press, 2014.

57   Spinoza is a lot more radical on this issue than his predecessors such as Moses Maimonides (Rambam), Hasdai Crescas, Abū l-Walīd Muhammad ibn Ahmad Ibn Rushd (Averroes), or Abū Alī al-Husain ibn Abd Allāh Ibn Sina (Avicenna).

58   Spinoza, E1p15.

59   Spinoza, E1d6, E4Pref.

60   Namita Goswami, *Subjects That Matter: Philosophy, Feminism and Postcolonial Theory*. New York: Suny Press, 2019, p. 149. See also Yitzhak Melamed, *Spinoza's Metaphysics: Substance and Thought*. Oxford: Oxford University Press, 2013, pp. 83–84.

actually heterogeneous with itself. Spinoza says it like this:

> [The] idea [of Joy or Sadness] is united to the affect in the same
> way as the Mind is united to the Body (by E2p21), i.e. (as I have
> shown in E2p21s), this idea is not really distinguished from
> the affect itself, or (by the general Definition of the Affects) from
> the idea of the Body's affection; *it is only conceptually distin-*
> *guished from it.* Therefore, this knowledge of good and evil
> is nothing but the affect itself, insofar as we are conscious of it
> [...].[61]

Here, Spinoza states that the idea of an affect or emotion *is really the*
same as the affect or emotion itself, mind and body are *really* the same,
and knowledge of good and evil are *really* just the conscious ideas of
joy and sadness, and consecutively nothing but joy and sadness themselves. The idea of an emotion is distinguished from that emotion *in*
the same way as the mind is distinguished from the body and *in the*
same way as good and evil are distinguished from joy and sadness:
They are *conceptually* distinct, but *not really*.

What, then, is a conceptual distinction? One example that Spinoza uses is the distinction between a circle and the idea of a circle:[62]
If we have a true idea of a circle, then whatever we *think* about that circle is an *aspect* of the circle, namely the form it takes in thought.[63] Of
course, circles are round whereas ideas of circles are not round. Thus,
the idea of the circle is not just *identical* with actually existing circles.
Simultaneously, however, the relation between a circle and the idea
of a circle is different from the relationship between my haircut and
me. I can exist with or without a fringe—the distinction here is modal
in that my haircut depends on me but not the other way around. But
the idea of a circle is hardwired into the circle. The distinction here
is conceptual.

---

61   Spinoza, E4p8d (my emphasis).
62   "For instance, a circle existing in nature, and the idea of a circle existing
     [...] are one and the same thing displayed through different attributes
     [such as thought or extension]." (Spinoza, E2p7s).
63   "A true idea must agree with its object" (Spinoza, E1a6); "in other words
     (obviously), that which is contained in the intellect objectively must
     necessarily be granted in nature." (Spinoza, E1p30d).

We may take mirror images and shadows as flawed analogies: Some things have mirror images and most mirror images have a parallel object in extension—but object and mirror image are nevertheless not the same. The one may well be perceived without the other, although they do not exist without the other completely—only vampires lack a mirror image. Likewise, if something casts a shadow, then that shadow is not without its thing and neither is that thing without its shadow, though both nevertheless may be discerned independently from each other. Yet again, only vampires lack a shadow. There are, however, no vampire-circles—circles without ideas of circles. Likewise, there are no *adequate* vampire-ideas—true ideas without some reference in external reality.

That does *not* mean that things like unicorns and triangles with four sides actually exist. After all, ideas may be constructed from disparate elements, of which each refers to something outside of thought, while their composition occurs only in thought. Spinoza calls these thoughts *chimeras*—unicorns (composed of horse and horn), four-sided-triangles (composed of square and triangle), and pure Nothingness (everything subtracted from something) are examples for chimeras. There is no space here for further elaboration on this.[64] The point is, however: There is a distinction that resides *between* real distinctions (things that are independent of each other in some relevant sense, such as epistemologically and ontologically),[65] on the one hand, and modal distinctions (things that are strictly dependent on other things—such as my haircut, which is strictly dependent on me), on the other. These distinctions are *conceptual* distinctions.

Borrowing Yitzhak Melamed's terminology, in these cases, we are talking about different *aspects* of a thing without numerical distinction.[66] My shadow and me, my mirror image and me, they do not

---

64 I elaborate on this, see Luce deLire, "Spinoza's Infinities," in Yitzhak Melamed (ed.), *Blackwell Companion to Philosophy: A Companion to Spinoza*. Oxford: Wiley Blackwell, 2021.

65 See Melamed, "The Building Blocks," for a contextualization of independence in Spinoza's theory with its Aristotelian and Cartesian counterparts.

66 See Melamed, "The Building Blocks"; Melamed, *Spinoza's Metaphysics*, pp. 83–84; Dobbs-Weinstein, *Spinoza's Critique of Religion*, p. 35; and Michael Della-Rocca, "The Elusiveness of the One and the Many in Spinoza: Substance, Attribute, and Mode," in Jack Stetter and Charles Ramond (eds), *Spinoza in Twenty-First-Century American and French*

count as two separate things. Yet simultaneously, I cannot change my mirror image as I can change my haircut. There are no mirror-dressers, as there are hairdressers. Nevertheless, although these aspects refer to the same thing, they cannot be reduced to one another. My mirror image and me can be perceived independently of each other (you may see one without the other) and do have different qualities (I weigh much more than my mirror image). The same counts for circles and the ideas of circles: The former are round, the latter are not. Spinoza would say the same about the distinction between body and mind. To Spinoza, the mind is nothing but the idea of a certain body (which is why trees, tigers, and tiaras have minds just as humans do). To Spinoza, the mind *is* the body in another dimension of reality and vice versa. Your body is the way in which you exist in extension; your mind is the way in which you exist in thought. My mind, then, is merely *conceptually distinct* from my body, just as the idea of a circle is merely *conceptually distinct* from an extended circle.[67]

The conceptual distinction *is real in the intellect*, because the intellect is itself an *aspect* of reality—the intellect genuinely perceives reality *in some way* (and nothing else).[68] Nevertheless, the intellect does not *produce* that difference (other than in the case of the chimera, see above). In this sense, me and my mirror image, a circle and the idea of it, a body and its mind are *heterogeneous* to one another: they behave in parallel ways, but reside in different realms. Each one is an *aspect* of a thing that, however, does not exist *beyond* its expressions. There are no pure mirror images in the world. In the same way, Spinoza says, any idea differs from its equivalent in extension—a certain body—merely *conceptually*. Bodies and their ideas are *aspects* of the

     Philosophy: Metaphysics, Philosophy of Mind, Moral and Political Philosophy. London: Bloomsbury Academic, 2019.

67   The same counts for the distinction between divine will and divine intellect (Spinoza, TTP, 1.23–25, II/62–63). In the *Ethics*, Spinoza will claim that God has neither will nor intellect (Spinoza, E2p48 and E2p49). See the distinctions between: the nexus of causes and the nexus of ideas (Spinoza, E2p7s); human desire and the human mind (Spinoza, E3DA1 and E2p13); thought and extension as dimensions of reality (Spinoza, E1p10s); and divine essence and divine existence (Spinoza, E1p20). In all of these cases, the distinction is *conceptual*, meaning that the distinction applies between *aspects* of the same thing, but not between actually independent things.

68   Spinoza, E1p30d.

same thing. This applies to the distinctions between minds and bodies, desires and minds, affects (joy/sadness) and ethical predicates (good/evil), true ideas and their objects, just as it applies to thought *in general* and extension *in general*.[69] In each case, these aspects are completely *heterogeneous* and have no bearing on one another. Here, the analogy with mirror images and shadows ends. For it is not *because* we manipulate the image of a circle in this or that way that its properties change. Both, however, may be manipulated in their own right and will nevertheless yield the same effects in (conceptually) different ways. If you manipulate the formula that describes a certain circle, you will get another circle or another figure altogether. But it does not require us to actually draw that figure in order for the formula to describe that figure. In the same way, Spinoza says, you do not act *because* of your thoughts, ideas are not true *because of* their referents, and you do not change your mind *because of* your desire. In each of these cases, the processes are strictly parallel *because* each side of the distinction each time is but an *aspect* of the same thing. This logic stretches even further. To Spinoza, essence, power, desire, and being are aspects of the same thing, as are perfection, reality, and causal force.[70]

Is there a thing beyond the aspects, a unity beyond the heterogeneity, and a reality beyond the distinction? For reasons that must remain unexplored in this text, the answer is "no." Reality necessarily splits into infinitely many irreducible expressions of the same thing plus their modes or affections. This is (maybe) the modernized sediment of that repressed "idiom"[71] of an Arabic Aristotelian materialism in Spinoza. If it is, then a history of violence—prohibition, omission, destruction of books—has rendered it barely readable. If it is not, then whatever remains unreadable about Spinoza's theory of distinctions experiences another violent bent—namely mine in this text.

There is no such thing as non-violent metaphysics. But there is metaphysics that embodies its material conditions and intervenes

69   Note that for Spinoza, there are infinitely many other attributes
      besides thought and extension. I will leave this aside for the moment.
      For a discussion of these matters, see Yitzhak Melamed, "Spinoza's
      Metaphysics of Substance," in Don Garrett (ed.), *Cambridge Companion
      to Spinoza*, 2nd ed., Cambridge: Cambridge University Press,
      forthcoming.forthcoming.
70   See Spinoza, E1p36d, E3p6d, and E4p4d.
71   Dobbs-Weinstein, *Spinoza's Critique of Religion*, p. 29.

instead of selling a product. There is violent metaphysics—the one that omits its material conditions and presents its results as commodities on the marketplace of ideas. And there is the metaphysics of violence which integrates its mode of production and appeals to its material and affective conditions, rather than to an imagined free subject that may choose to accept or reject allegedly useful theoretical tools at will. Otherwise said: There is the metaphysics of real distinctions, where the mind is severed from the body and its desires, its affective landscapes, where theories are imagined as innocent frameworks for future applications. And there is the metaphysics of conceptual distinctions, where mind and body are *aspects* of the same thing, affect and desire are corporeal expressions equal to their parallel thoughts, while theories are real manifestations and integral *aspects* of material conditions, interventions rather than descriptions. This intervention is philosophy as a *practice* and not an endeavor contained in institutions and reading circles, nor geared towards future *applications. Doing philosophy* is its own application already. Likewise, every practice produces its *philosophy*, no matter how strong the will to deny this parallel expression in thought may be. Violence remains inevitable—but there are different ways of staging it.

The Heterogeneity
of the Internet

The heterogeneity of reality is crucial for the understanding of knowledge production in the twenty-first century, as digitalization revolutionizes both knowledge and identity.[72] Spinoza could not have foreseen this development. What could Spinoza say about digitalization? He could mark the *conceptual distinctions* at work.

---

72   "Land is the detachment of a resource from nature [qua absolutely infinite reality], an *aspect* of the productive potential of nature rendered abstract, in the form of property. Capital is the detachment of a resource from land, an *aspect* of the productive potential of land rendered abstract in the form of property. Information is the detachment of a resource from capital already detached from land. It is the double of a double. It is a further process of abstraction beyond capital, but one that yet again produces its separate existence in the form of property." (McKenzie Wark, *A Hacker Manifesto*. Cambridge, MA: Harvard University Press, 2004, paragraphs 017, my emphasis).

Alyk Blue, *We Overlap*, from the series „Connections", 2020

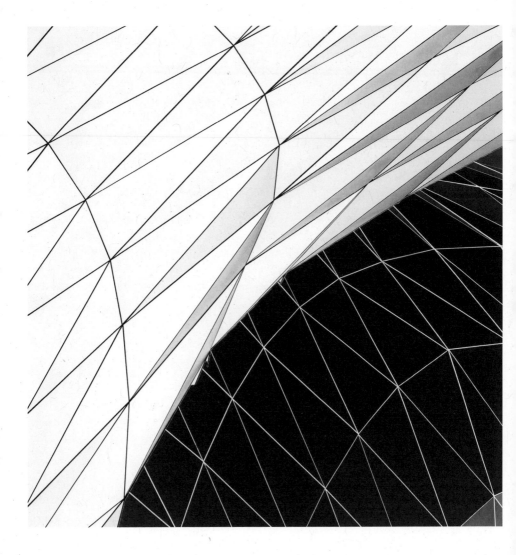

Alyk Blue, *We Overlap II*, from the series „Connections", 2020

Let us start with Internet architecture: Online distance is measured in clicks—it takes me one click to get into my email account, but fifteen to reach an Alt-Right board on 4chan. The Internet is built around personal devices and based on the logic of capitalism: Accumulation of capital is achieved by the accumulation of clicks and accumulation of time spent at the same place. The Internet wants you to click more and spend more time in it. Therefore, the magic algorithms of the Internet produce a differently shaped online architecture for every user, according to the likeliness of that user to spend time and clicks. My Internet is thus *conceptually different* from your Internet: they are *aspects* of the Internet. However, even if there were a bird's-eye view, it would be just another aspect. The Internet is not a quasi-universal,[73] nor a virtual-qua-deferred-actuality,[74] but a heterogeneous structure. In other words: Digital reality is heterogenous reality. Although based on binary *coding*, the internet as an aspect of reality does *not* obey binary determinations such as "online/offline," "actual/virtual," or "universal/particular."

[73]   Paradigmatically: "The flat-world platform is the product of a convergence of the personal computer (which allowed every individual suddenly to become the author of his or her own content in digital form) with fiber-optic cable (which suddenly allowed all those individuals to access more and more digital content around the world for next to nothing) with the rise of workflow software (which enabled individuals all over the world to collaborate on that same digital content from anywhere, regardless of the distances between them). No one anticipated this convergence. It just happened—right around the year 2000." (Thomas L. Friedman, *The World is Flat: A Brief History of the Twenty-First Century.* New York: Picador, 2007, pp. 10-11). Alternatively, in a more contemporary version of this: "It is evident that the digital culture cannot be perceived as a particular realm; symbiotic relationships are being forged, one could even claim that entire ecologies are emerging from these coevolutionary processes." (Bernd Scherer, "Cosmology of Perspectives and Digital Code," in Bernd Scherer (ed.), *The New Alphabet.* Leipzig: Spector Books, 2021, p. 34).

[74]   For example: "To the hacker there is always a surplus of possibility expressed in what is actual, the surplus of the virtual. This is the inexhaustible domain of what is real, but not actual, what is not but which may become. […] To hack is to release the virtual into the actual [and thus proclaim the primacy of the actual over the virtual], to express the difference of the real." (See Wark, *Hacker Manifesto,* paragraph 074).

This is important in the case of the geopolitical location of the hetero-geneous Internet. For one, language remains a differentiating factor within the Internet—quality journalism in English on local issues in Athens or Berlin is hard to come by and political conversations often remain bound to national languages. Next, there are various sub-Webs. Most obviously, the Big Firewall seals off the Chinese Web from its counterparts. This counts for the North Korean Web as well.[75] Moreover, the location of physical servers sets the legal agenda at play in cyberspace. Most, although by no means all, Internet servers reside in the USA, making them susceptible to US jurisdiction. Additional legal frameworks may apply, such as the long arm of the German GEMA,[76] which may at times restrict access to platforms that facili-tate the distribution of videos or other media. Lastly, the transatlantic online connection is physically wired through a single gigantic cable, which Western powers protect and intercept by all possible means.

TL;DR: The Internet appears unified under neoliberal capital-ism, but conceptually distinguished between users and peer groups, asymmetrically defined by physical location, and subject to various jurisdictions, languages, and online architectures. There is thus not *one* Internet. The Internet is in fact not itself—it is *heterogeneous*. The fantasy of a universal framework only serves to omit the real geopolit-ical conflicts that happen on the ground. The term "World Wide Web" is a purely ideological slogan.

The same counts for digitalized identity: Your online presence is only *conceptually distinct* from your off-line life. In this sense, your presence online is yet another, conceptually distinct *aspect* of you, distinct only inasmuch as your mind is *conceptually distinct* from your body. Your online trace is like a shadow, a mirror image or the idea of an object—it is hardwired into your existence, may be conceptualized independently, but does not refer to a numerically different object, person, or body. That is why cancel culture is real violence, why social media is a real transformation of the political sphere, and harvesting

---

75   See for example, Mark Lechtik, 35C3 - *SiliVaccine: North Korea's Weapon of Mass Detection* [video, uploaded 27 December 2018], https://www.youtube.com/watch?v=7xcLAiWQm9Y, accessed October 26, 2020.
76   GEMA: Gesellschaft für musikalische Aufführungs- und mechanische Vervielfältigungsrechte (Society for musical performing and mechanical reproduction rights).

data is real exploitation. It was and is a principal error of our time to understand "online" to mean "accidental," "modal," or "not-real." This metaphysical confusion has provided the grounds for the large-scale and almost unchecked intrusion of capitalist enterprises into this new aspect or dimension of reality and the violence that comes with it—the colonization and original accumulation of cyberspace.[77]

Reality is not pure immanence, but the inevitable deflection of heterogeneous aspects into one another. With Spivak, we may call the move from one aspect to another a *coding* and *re-coding*. In fact, your Internet and my Internet are differently *coded* (for example through online architecture, legal framework etc.). In the same way, reality is differently *coded* in corporeal and intellectual perception, just as political discourses may be differently *coded* under economic, libidinal, or genealogical *aspects*.[78] A discourse, in fact, may be understood as a *coding* of reality that is in itself infinite—the language of economy captures *all of reality,* just as the language of desire, the language of imperialism, the language of culture wars, etc., etc. Note that none of these *codings* are partial—each one of them captures *all of reality under a different aspect* or in a different *dimension* and without restrictions. There is nothing beyond these expressions, no underlying reality that was to be discovered beyond its aspects. However, "[b]y the time one gets to call [...] [these *codings*] anything—capital, or nature, or despot—a good deal of inaccessible coding has already taken place. [...]. For there is of course a tremendous political difference between the name being capital, or despot, or yet nature."[79] Consequentially, the concrete conditions of those *living inside the problems* of particularly *coded* discursive fields—economy, psychology, desire—must take precedence in political action over everything else.

Conclusion

In this text, I have tried to exemplify a materialistic theory of knowledge as violent metaphysics. We have shown that the European Enlightenment was deeply shaped by Spinoza and that the latter

77   See Ziauddin Sardar, "alt.civilizations.faq: Cyberspace as the darker side of the West," *Futures*, vol. 27, no. 7 (September 1995), pp. 777-94.
78   Spivak, *A Critique of Postcolonial Reason*, p. 104.
79   Ibid., p. 106.

occupies a number of deflecting social positions—Jew, Atheist, Christian, Oriental, Modern. The violence articulated in these terms is constitutive of Spinoza's philosophy and not external to it. I have tried to articulate a layer of this philosophy that is covered by protective devices, namely the heterogeneity of reality with itself. I have then exemplified this theory in the case of the Internet as a primary means of knowledge production in the twenty-first century.

To conclude, I want to reiterate that practice is not an application of theory, nor can the one do without the other. Both are *aspects of the same thing*, which, however, does not exist beyond its expressions in theory and in practice and in theory as practice and in practice as theory (of theory and of practice), etc., etc. Of this, I hope, this text may function as an expression.

---

*   As is customary and to ensure adequate references across editions and translations, I quote Spinoza as follows: References to the *Theologico-Political Treatise* are marked as TTP, followed by the number of the chapter and the number of the paragraph within the chapter. TTP 10.1 refers to chapter 10, first paragraph. References to the *Ethics* commence with an E (for *Ethics*), followed by the number of the chapter, and further specifications. E1p10s refers to *Ethics*, chapter one, proposition 10, scholium. E3DA1 stands for *Ethics*, chapter three, definition of affects number one, etc. "Ep." stands for "letter" (Ep. 68 is letter number 68). Where necessary, I will add the so-called "Gebhardt numbers," referring to the standard edition in Latin: Carl Gebhardt (ed.), *Spinoza: Opera* (originally 4 vols, Heidelberg: Carl Winter-Verlag, 1925; second edition Heidelberg: Carl Winter-Verlag, 1973). For example, II / 37 / 10–15 refers to the second volume of the Gebhardt edition, page 37, lines 10–15. Most modern translations (in all languages) print the Gebhardt numbers alongside the translated text, such that a general orientation despite languages and editions should be easily possible. Note that my English versions of the text are mostly my own translations from Gebhardt's Latin edition. However, for the modern Standard English edition of the text, see Edwin Curley (ed.), *The Collected Works of Spinoza, Volume 1*. Princeton, NJ: Princeton University Press, 1985; and Edwin Curley (ed.), *The Collected Works of Spinoza, Volume 2*. Princeton, NJ: Princeton University Press, 2016. The *Ethics* can be found in the first volume of that edition, as can letters 1–28. The TTP can be found in the second volume of that edition, as can letters 29–84.

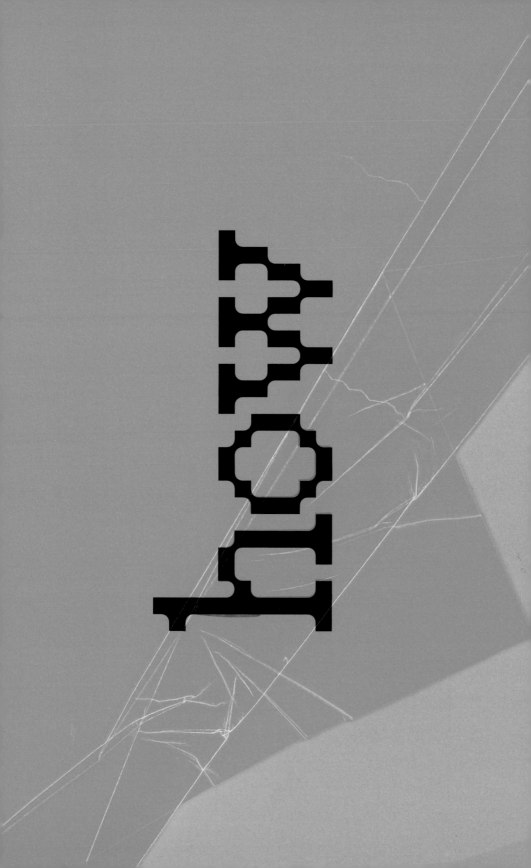

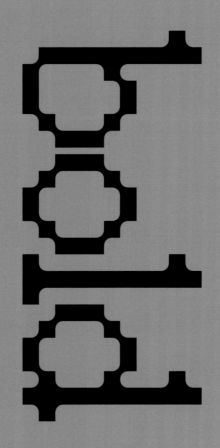

If not otherwise noted, translations from German and Latin are mine.

Many thanks to: Till Bardoux, Helmut Draxler, Mandi Gomez, Kyla Greenhalgh, Martin Hager, Namita Goswami, Gilah Kletenik, Yitzhak Melamed, Daniel Neugebauer, Martin Saar, and Danny Schwartz.

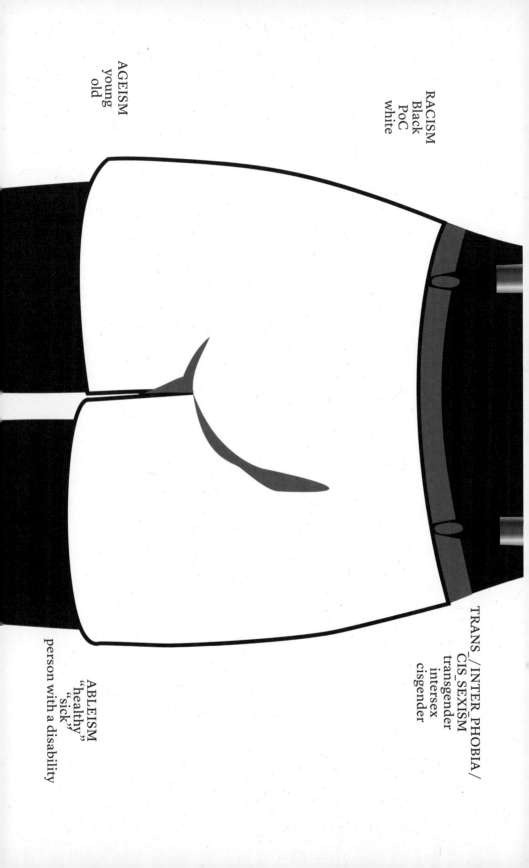

AGEISM
young
old

RACISM
Black
PoC
white

TRANS_/INTER PHOBIA /
CIS_SEXISM
transgender
intersex
cisgender

ABLEISM
"healthy"
"sick"
person with a disability

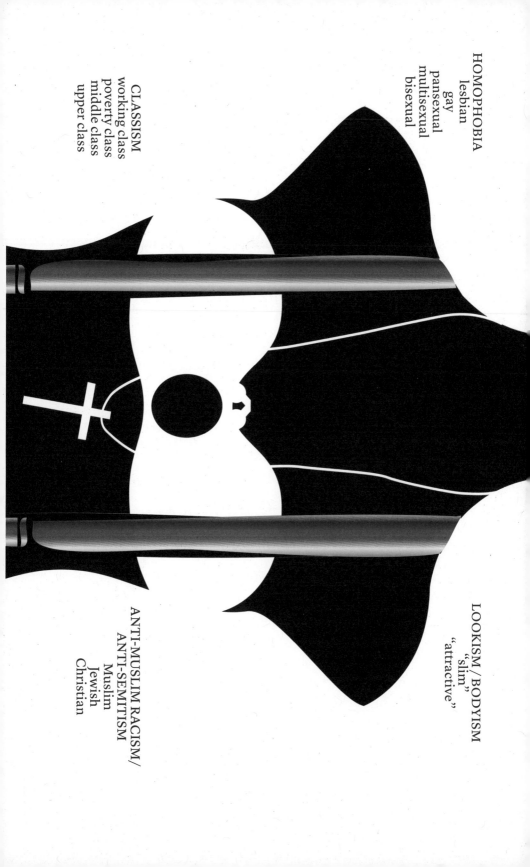

HOMOPHOBIA
lesbian
gay
pansexual
multisexual
bisexual

CLASSISM
working class
poverty class
middle class
upper class

LOOKISM/BODYISM
"slim"
"attractive"

ANTI-MUSLIM RACISM/
ANTI-SEMITISM
Muslim
Jewish
Christian

METHOD: DENIZ

This method seeks to raise self-awareness and awareness about an individual's perception of others, to sensitize participants to different factors of identity and the ways these interact in various mechanisms of oppression within society. It also encourages participants to think about perceptions and norms, and shows how we all use categorical thinking to classify other people.

Framework

Duration: 75 min

Group: 12–20 participants aged 12 and older

Materials: Flip chart, pens, a mannequin (perhaps a "female" torso; these are available from multiple Internet sources for approx. €25)

Location: The space should be large enough for participants to sit in a circle

Objectives: ▪ Sensitization to different identity factors and their evaluation
              ▪ Reflection on societal norms and "deviations" from these norms
              ▪ Increased awareness of the power relations that exist within society
              ▪ Sensitization to different forms of discrimination and oppression
              ▪ Elucidation of the relationship between self-awareness and the perception of others, and of the link between prejudices and stereotypes, with regard to individual features such as clothing, habitus, subculture, etc.

Preparation

Before the workshop begins, the mannequin "Deniz" is placed on one of the chairs in the circle. Deniz is dressed in a carefully chosen outfit: a close-fitting top and threadbare underpants/boxer shorts with a padded crotch. The underpants are held up by rainbow-colored suspenders, to which a politically themed badge (related to a political party or a particular organization) is pinned. Deniz wears a crucifix around their neck and—like all the other members of the group—they are wearing a name tag.

The exercise

The leader of the group introduces "Deniz," who has been placed on one of the chairs in the circle since the workshop began, to the other participants. They are asked to look at Deniz and choose an item they would like to give them for the rest of the day. Each member of the group is then asked to give Deniz (or dress them in) the item they think Deniz could use. These items might include paper handkerchiefs, cellphones, water, books, toys, condoms, or articles of clothing—there are no "right" or "wrong" items here. After all the participants have given Deniz something, each individual is asked to explain why they chose that particular item. Each person is then invited to share with the group what goes through their mind when they look at Deniz. The various features named by the participants are assigned to different categories (e.g. ability, religion, class), and the group members then define and discuss what is considered to be the "norm" in Germany within these categories, and what is regarded as a "deviation" from the norm.

Based upon the respective distinguishing features, Deniz is situated within each of these contexts. Deniz's distinguishing features are noted down on a flip chart or whiteboard and the participants jointly assign them to the different categories being evaluated. Examples of this process include:

Chains of association for use in compiling categories

Deniz's distinguishing features	Interpretations	Category
rainbow-colored suspenders	LGBTQI symbol, gay, lesbian	sexual orientation
threadbare underpants	possible sign of poverty /hardship	social status/class
visible breasts and male genitalia	intersex person, personal pronoun	gender identity
characteristics of gender	gender roles, personal pronoun	gender
missing limbs	disability	physical ability
	disability	mental and intellectual capacity
slim, athletic body	young, sporty, dynamic	body
slim, athletic body	young, wrinkle-free skin, healthy appearance	age
black mannequin	Black person	being white, being Black, being a person of color
crucifix, cross	religious, Roman Catholic	religion, worldview

and noting Deniz's distinguishing features

Norm	"Deviation"	Form of discrimination
heterosexual	homosexual, bisexual, multisexual, pansexual	homophobia
middle class	working class, poverty class	classism
cisgender	transgender or intersex	cissexism, transphobia
man	woman	sexism
person without a disability	person with a disability	ableism
"healthy"	"sick"	ableism
"slim" and "attractive"	"fat," "unkempt," and "unattractive"	lookism, bodyism, fat phobia
young adults, people aged between 25 and 45	children, adolescents, and elderly people	ageism, adultism
white people	Black people, people of color	racism
Christian, secular	non-Christian, e.g. Muslim, Jewish, Buddhist	anti-Muslim racism, anti-Semitism

During the evaluation and reflection phase, an opportunity for moderated discussion should be provided. Differences of opinion and perspective can generate controversial debate. As it is not possible to address every aspect of the subject under discussion, a specific focus should be established in relation to the target group. Smaller group work may take place for a more detailed analysis.

Conclusion

It is important for the exercise to be brought to a joint conclusion with Deniz as they have become part of the group and part of the histories of all those involved. The participants can now either bid farewell to Deniz or keep them within the group. The way in which individuals bid farewell to Deniz can vary according to the mood of the group. For example, each person could take an item and, on behalf of Deniz, thank the person who gave it and explain why they are grateful for it. Deniz can, however, also stay with the group and accompany the ongoing process. This makes it possible for Deniz to be involved again at a later stage.

Translated from the German by Jacqueline Todd

*   The Initiative intersektionale Pädagogik (Initiative for Intersectional Pedagogy – i-PÄD) was founded in 2011 in Berlin. An interdisciplinary team—of educators, social workers, political scientists, and psychologists—has developed materials and workshops for schools and other educational establishments with the aim to increase awareness of the complexity of human identities within pedagogical practice.

What action strategies are required in order to facilitate prejudice-conscious education? How can professionals in teaching sensitize themselves to invisible discrimination? How can we gain greater understanding of the fact that children and young people, as well as educators, have multiple identity factors, and what are particularly effective means in the fight against exclusion?

The i-PÄD brochure on intersectional pedagogy includes teaching methods, interviews, a glossary, and observations drawn from firsthand experience. The description of the "Deniz" method is taken from this brochure, available at www.i-paed-berlin.de.

Julia Velkova, Anne Kaun

Algorithmic Resistance:
Media Practices and the Politics of Repair

The Drama of Algorithmic Culture

The subject of user agency is often neglected in the emerging discussion of the consequences of algorithmic culture, which increasingly is wrapped in a narrative of drama. Scholars, journalists, and citizens alike have raised concerns about the closing off and isolation of digital public spheres by a number of means. For example, through divisions generated by preemptive taste management curated by algorithmic logics;[1] the reproduction of biases against race and gender in search engine algorithms;[2] and the suppression of ethics and the management of everyday experience in favor of commercial logics based on the politics of satisfaction and normalization of the average.[3] As algorithms assume a dominant role in the mediation of power, it becomes increasingly important to consider to what extent and in what ways their power can be resisted. Hence, this essay engages with mundane user encounters with algorithms that can be inspirational for political projects which embrace—rather than denounce—the algorithmic power embedded in platforms and channel it to both serve specific political ends and act upon biased algorithmic output.

The extent to which power and biases are embedded in and run through technologies like algorithms might appear to be a novelty. As such, the possibilities to object to such power could seem out of reach for ordinary users. Yet, debates about the social construction of technology, which played out already in the 1980s, refused deterministic accounts of technological diffusion and made clear that, despite technology representing one of the major sources of power in modern societies, practices of use can alter its dominant social meanings and

---

1   Jeremy Wade Morris, "Curation by Code: Infomediaries and the Data Mining of Taste," *European Journal of Cultural Studies*, vol. 18, nos 4–5 (2015), pp. 446–63.

2   Safiya Umoja Noble, *Algorithms of Oppression: How Search Engines Reinforce Racism*. New York: New York University Press, 2018.

3   Mike Ananny, "Toward an Ethics of Algorithms: Convening, Observation, Probability, and Timeliness," *Science, Technology, & Human Values*, vol. 41, no. 1 (2016), pp. 93–117.

add variety to prescribed uses embedded in technological design.[4] Indeed, it is well known that designers project specific meanings onto technologies under development, "configuring" imagined and idealized users.[5] At the other end of the scale, users also negotiate the meaning and functionality of technologies by making multiple use of them in ways that may either comply with or deviate from the "original" meanings envisioned by designers.[6]

By acknowledging the mutual co-construction of algorithms with their users, and by zooming into some of the alternative uses of algorithms, we reframe the public and academic debates on algorithmic power, which have taken a rather dystopian turn of late grounded in an instrumentalist understanding of technology. As a way of balancing thought with the growing literature that discusses the power of algorithms, this essay, instead, locates the possibilities for agency and algorithmic resistance within practices of use of the platforms within which algorithms are embedded. Specifically, we foreground the significance of mundane user encounters with algorithms whereby users can develop tactics[7] of resistance by making alternative use of them. These tactics can be based on users complying with algorithmic logics but resisting their output, "tricking" algorithms to work toward unintended ends through what we call "repair politics," or the politics of

4   Wiebe E. Bijker, Thomas P. Hughes, and Trevor Pinch (eds), *The Social Construction of Technological Systems: New Directions in the Sociology and History of Technology*. Cambridge, MA: MIT Press, 1987; Andrew Feenberg, *Transforming Technology: A Critical Theory Revisited*. New York: Oxford University Press, 2002; and Donald MacKenzie and Judy Wajcman (eds), *The Social Shaping of Technology*, 2nd ed. Buckingham and Philadelphia, PA: Open University Press, 1999.
5   Anne M. Balsamo, *Designing Culture: The Technological Imagination at Work*. Durham, NC: Duke University Press, 2011; Bonnie A. Nardi, *A Small Matter of Programming: Perspectives on End User Computing*. Cambridge, MA: MIT Press, 1993; Langdon Winner, "Do Artifacts have Politics?," in MacKenzie and Wajcman (eds), *The Social Shaping of Technology*, 1999, pp. 28–40; and Steve Woolgar, "Configuring the User: The Case of Usability Trials," *The Sociological Review*, vol. 38 (May 1990), pp. 58–99.
6   Andrew Feenberg and Alastair Hannay (eds), *Technology and the Politics of Knowledge*. Bloomington, IN: Indiana University Press, 1995; and Nelly Oudshoorn and Trevor Pinch (eds), *How Users Matter: The Co-Construction of Users and Technologies*. Cambridge, MA: MIT Press, 2003.
7   Michel de Certeau, *The Practice of Everyday Life*. Berkeley, CA: University of California Press, 1984.

partial and improvisational correction of biased results of algorithmic work. By foregrounding some of the ways in which "repair politics" can be performed, we contribute to an epistemological reframing of the debate on algorithms, through which we can start charting more hopeful approaches to managing their power in everyday life.

Algorithmic Power and the Politics of Algorithmic Use

Algorithms have always been an intrinsic part of digital media and information technologies. However, given the increasing role that they have come to play in structuring everyday online communication, in organizing and recommending media content, or exercising the power to make decisions in areas such as public administration, their power over the self and society has grown tremendously.[8] At the same time, ontologically, their presence and governing capacities seem to have remained invisible and impossible to penetrate, provoking what some have termed "a crisis of control."[9]

Algorithms form part of the "technological unconscious"[10] that underpins the fabric of social life, while their logics most often remain

8   Mike Ananny and Kate Crawford, "Seeing without Knowing: Limitations of the Transparency Ideal and its Application to Algorithmic Accountability," *New Media & Society*, vol. 20, no. 3 (2018), pp. 973–89; David G. Beer, "The Social Power of Algorithms," *Information, Communication & Society*, vol. 20, no. 1 (2017), pp. 1–13; Zi Chu, Steven Gianvecchio, Haining Wang, et al., "Who is Tweeting on Twitter: Human, Bot, or Cyborg?," in *Proceedings of the 26th Annual Computer Security Applications Conference*. New York: ACM, 2010, pp. 21–30; Tarleton Gillespie, "The Relevance of Algorithms," in Tarleton Gillespie, Pablo. J. Boczkowski, and Kristen A. Foot (eds), *Media Technologies: Essays on Communication, Materiality, and Society*. Cambridge, MA: MIT Press, 2014, pp. 167–94, and Rob Kitchin, "Thinking Critically About and Researching Algorithms," *Information, Communication & Society*, vol. 20, no. 1 (2017), pp. 14–29.

9   Balázs Bodó, Natali Helberger, Kristina Irion, et al., "Tackling the Algorithmic Control Crisis: The Technical, Legal, and Ethical Challenges of Research into Algorithmic Agents," *Yale Journal of Law and Technology*, vol. 19, no. 1 (2018), pp. 133–82, http://digitalcommons.law.yale.edu/yjolt/vol19/iss1/3, accessed November 6, 2020.

10 Nigel Thrift, "Remembering the Technological Unconscious by Foregrounding Knowledges of Position," in Nigel Thrift (ed.), *Knowing Capitalism*. London: Sage Publications, 2005, pp. 212–26.

black-boxed and difficult to trace or question.[11] The invisibility of the structuring power of algorithms is a key feature that has been argued to represent a new form of hegemonic power operating on the basis of generative rules, or "virtuals that generate a whole variety of actuals."[12] Scott Lash explains that the logics of code which are embedded in algorithms act as conduits of capitalist power, making power increasingly embedded in the algorithm. As such, for Lash power in society becomes ontological, embedded in code, and hence more difficult to object to, subvert, or undermine by means that have traditionally been used against hegemonies. One consequence of such a reorientation of power has been the eclipse of the commonly acclaimed participatory potential of social media and online spaces in favor of its algorithmic regulation.[13] An urgent question for researchers became to understand how the new forms of algorithmic governance operate, for example, by studying their ethics[14] and ways of creating accountability,[15] or by elaborating methods to study algorithms in the first place.[16] The scholarly concern with the power and workings of

---

11   Kitchin, "Thinking Critically About and Researching Algorithms"; Frank
      Pasquale, *The Black Box Society: The Secret Algorithms that Control
      Money and Information.* Cambridge, MA: Harvard University Press, 2015.
12   Scott Lash, "Power after Hegemony: Cultural Studies in Mutation?,"
      Theory, Culture & Society, vol. 24, no. 3 (2007), pp. 55–78, here p. 71.
13   David Beer, "Power through the Algorithm? Participatory Web Cultures
      and the Technological Unconscious," *New Media & Society*, vol. 11,
      no. 6 (2009), pp. 985–1002; and Ganaele Langlois, "Participatory Culture
      and the New Governance of Communication: The Paradox of Partic-
      ipatory Media," *Television & New Media*, vol. 14, no. 2 (2013), pp. 91–105.
14   Ananny, "Toward an Ethics of Algorithms."
15   Christian Sandvig, Kevin Hamilton, Karrie Karahalios, et al., "When
      the Algorithm Itself is a Racist: Diagnosing Ethical Harm in the Basic
      Components of Software," *International Journal of Communications*,
      vol. 10 (January 2016), pp. 4972–90, http://ijoc.org/index.php/ijoc/
      article/view/6182/1807, accessed November 6, 2020.
16   Taina Bucher, "Neither Black nor Box: Ways of Knowing Algorithms," in
      Sebastian Kubitschko and Anne Kaun (eds), *Innovative Methods in
      Media and Communication Research.* Cham: Palgrave Macmillan, 2016,
      pp. 81–98; Kitchin, "Thinking Critically About and Researching Algo-
      rithms"; and Nick Seaver, "Knowing Algorithms," paper presented
      at "Media in Transition", April 8, 2013, Cambridge, MA [online, revised
      February 2014], https://nick-seaver.squarespace.com/s/seaverMiT8.pdf,
      accessed November 6, 2020.

algorithms has shown that this power lies as much in their code as in the meanings that algorithms are attributed in society. These meanings can vary broadly—from the ontological definition of algorithms and the production of their authority[17] to the ways in which their production impacts the present and the future. Future-oriented concerns are almost exclusively related to the automation of work and crucial societal functions in ways that cannot live up to democratic, modernist ideals of transparency.[18] In this context, Ned Rossiter and Soenke Zehle have rightfully raised the question about what could constitute political action when disruption is seemingly absorbed as a normative condition within systems of calculation and control that render resistance futile.[19] Whereas this critical body of scholarship has defined algorithms as objects to fear, a pressing question is still the extent to which everyday media users are only subjects and victims of algorithmic power. Are they so powerless against the workings of algorithms?

Algorithmic power, no matter how obscure, is geared toward evaluating and regulating what becomes visible and what remains out of sight, and to whom.[20] This particular regulatory logic, regardless of the specificity of the computational media within which it is embedded, ultimately resembles the logic of traditional media, such as publishers, libraries, and broadcasters, which have the ability to amplify or suppress voices.[21] Hence, the dominant politics through which algorithmic power functions is an attention politics that defines dominant meanings and representations of objects, people, and events.

17   Beer, "The Social Power of Algorithms"; Kitchin, "Thinking Critically About and Researching Algorithms"; Caitlin Lustig and Bonnie Nardi, "Algorithmic Authority: The Case of Bitcoin," in *Proceedings of the 48th Annual Hawaii International Conference on System Sciences*, 5–8 January 2015. Hawaii: IEEE, 2015, pp. 743–52; and Adrian Mackenzie, *Cutting Code: Software and Sociality*. New York: Peter Lang, 2006.
18   Ananny and Crawford, "Seeing without Knowing."
19   Ned Rossiter and Soenke Zehle, "The Aesthetics of Algorithmic Experience," in Randy Martin (ed.), *The Routledge Companion to Art and Politics*. London and New York: Routledge, 2015, pp. 214–21.
20   Taina Bucher, "Want to be on the Top? Algorithmic Power and the Threat of Invisibility on Facebook," *New Media & Society*, vol. 14, no. 7 (2012), pp. 1164–80.
21   Tarleton Gillespie, "Algorithmically Recognizable: Santorum's Google Problem, and Google's Santorum Problem," *Information, Communication & Society*, vol. 20, no. 1 (2017), pp. 63–80, here p. 75.

What counts as worth being promoted or demoted by algorithms is shaped in a complex interplay between them and users. Algorithms are dependent on users for the queries that make them work and for the generation of data. User-generated data must be produced and aggregated so that algorithms can start to "define which information is to be included in an analysis; [and] envision, plan for, and execute data transformations."[22] Users are not passive observers in this process. They increasingly recognize the role they play in shaping the workings of algorithms, and they have begun to strategically intervene in political, commercial, or playful ways in the algorithmic politics of attention. For example, the growing industry of search engine optimization caters to the need of businesses to stay on top of algorithmic visibility logics.[23] New content producers, such as influencers and online celebrities, are also finding increasing possibilities to stimulate or boost their popularity within the regulatory structure of algorithms on platforms such as Instagram.[24] Often, as Kelly Cotter argues, influencers feel an obligation to know how algorithms work in order to be able to be part of the "visibility game" and to engage in gearing algorithmic workings toward their own benefit; this manifests, for instance, in crafting an influencer online identity. Just as algorithms study user behavior to promote commercial interests, users study algorithmic behavior in order to advance their own interests.

In some cases, these interests can be geared toward the development of identity and taste, rather than toward commercial practices. In the context of everyday practices such as mundane music listening, users embrace algorithms in what some have called "a symbiotic relationship,"[25] in which users relate to algorithms as companions and advisors that can help them to cultivate their taste in music. At the same time, in such relationships algorithms may also take advantage of users by imposing ideas of neoliberal productivity

22   Ananny, "Toward an Ethics of Algorithms," p. 98.
23   Nora A. Draper, *The Identity Trade: Selling Privacy and Reputation Online*. New York: New York University Press, 2019.
24   Kelly Cotter, "Playing the Visibility Game: How Digital Influencers and Algorithms Negotiate Influence on Instagram," *New Media & Society*, vol. 21, no. 4 (2018), pp. 895–913.
25   Nedim Karakayali, Burc Kostem, and Idil Galip, "Recommendation Systems as Technologies of the Self: Algorithmic Control and the Formation of Music Taste," *Theory, Culture & Society*, vol. 35, no. 2 (2018), pp. 3–24.

through music-recommendation systems.[26] In yet other cases, mundane encounters with algorithms can provoke users to develop tactics to trick algorithms to work toward unintended ends.[27] Such acts can have profound effects when put to use by political activists, as demonstrated by an activist campaign that promoted alternative meanings of US Senator Rick Santorum's name for more than a decade in Google's search results.[28] Algorithmic power can be further resisted through activist techno-political practices, or algorithmic activism,[29] as demonstrated in examples of the Indignados anti-austerity movement in Spain, who design complete media ecologies of independent outlets and platforms, ranging from websites to independent social networking sites. Activist work also exploits existing algorithms, like Twitter, to achieve goals of resistance, increasing the visibility of political causes without challenging the algorithmic logic as such.[30]

Algorithmic systems amplify or suppress voices. Therefore, for a plethora of users who struggle for online visibility, or who work with algorithms to develop their identities and tastes, they have become both an arena and an object for political efforts. Hence, in order to expand our understandings of the power of algorithms and the possibilities of user agency to act on this power, we must recognize the myriad of practices through which people act with and on digital technologies and infrastructures. Rob Kitchin has suggested that studies of algorithmic production need to focus not only on the contexts where algorithms are designed but also on the plethora of situations in which people "resist, subvert and transgress against the work of algorithms, and re-purpose and re-deploy them for purposes they were not originally intended."[31] Resistance against and subversion

---

26   Maria Eriksson and Anna Johansson, "'Keep Smiling!': Time, Functionality and Intimacy in Spotify's Featured Playlists," *Cultural Analysis*, vol. 16, no. 1 (2017), pp. 67–82.

27   Taina Bucher, "The Algorithmic Imaginary: Exploring the Ordinary Affects of Facebook Algorithms," *Information, Communication & Society*, vol. 20, no. 1 (2017), pp. 30–44.

28   Gillespie, "Algorithmically Recognizable."

29   Emiliano Treré, Sandra Jeppesen, and Alice Mattoni, "Comparing Digital Protest Media Imaginaries: Anti-Austerity Movements in Spain, Italy and Greece," *tripleC: Communication, Capitalism & Critique*, vol. 15, no. 2 (2017), pp. 404–22.

30   Ibid.

31   Kitchin, "Thinking Critically About and Researching Algorithms."

of the dominant logics of algorithmic governance tend to happen precisely by means of users mobilizing algorithms toward ends that were not originally intended, ultimately directing the politics of attention toward other objects that users might consider more important to be amplified than those that have been calculated by algorithms as deserving attention.

Locating User Agency: Algorithms as Technologies

Few authors involved in the debate about algorithms conceptualize them in terms of technologies. More often, their ontology is thought of in relation to code, sociotechnical assemblages, as imaginaries, or as conduits of power. Malte Ziewitz summarizes the definitional problem of algorithms with the comment that "we don't know [what an algorithm is], but surely it is very powerful."[32] A fruitful way of addressing this issue is to return to the more established and conventional understanding of algorithms as technologies; as Nick Seaver points out, this is also the way that key textbooks introduce algorithms to computer science students.[33] Furthermore, following Philip Napoli's proposal that some algorithms can be conceptualized as media institutions,[34] it should not be perceived as uncommon that they can be resisted, subverted, and questioned by the broader public. After all, processes of public institutional criticism have been at the core of liberal democracy for decades.

Hacking, technological disruption, and obfuscation could be some of the paths through which the functioning and purpose of technologies are redefined, collectively and politically. But technopolitics can also be exercised through media practices.

Recent developments in media theory that have embraced and developed further the "practice turn" from sociology have increasingly acknowledged the breadth of media practices through which

32   Malte Ziewitz, "Governing Algorithms: Myth, Mess, and Methods," *Science, Technology, & Human Values*, vol. 41, no. 1 (2016), pp. 3–16, here p. 6.
33   Seaver, "Knowing Algorithms."
34   Philip M. Napoli, "Automated Media: An Institutional Theory Perspective on Algorithmic Media Production and Consumption," *Communication Theory*, vol. 24, no. 3 (2014), pp. 340–60.

users can act on technologies and infrastructures. The analysis of media practice is loosely defined as the study of human action in relation to media across a whole range of situations and contexts.[35] Media practices stand for "what people are doing in relation to media in the contexts in which they act."[36]

Indeed, as Roger Silverstone and Leslie Haddon have argued, the emerging character of a new technology is shaped both by the intentions of designers who "configure"[37] users by creating mental maps of their potential engagements with a technical object and by users' actual practices, which are influenced by the social, cultural, and economic contexts within which they are situated.[38] By analogy, even though algorithms are designed to have governing capacities and to orient users toward specific modes of engagements with the platforms within which algorithms operate, it is impossible to determine and fully predict the ways in which users might employ algorithms or give them a different meaning and function than prescribed by their designers. In order to understand sociotechnical change, it becomes important to analyze the forms that such resistance can take.

The World White Web Project

In 2015, Swedish design student Johanna Burai needed an image of a hand for a graphic design assignment. She did the most obvious thing and turned to Google's image search, but was struck by the results, which consisted only of white hands or pictograms. At first, she assumed that it was her location in Sweden that had led to a personalized, overwhelmingly white search result, so she asked a friend,

35   Birgit Bräuchler and John Postill (eds), *Theorising Media and Practice.* New York: Berghahn Books, 2010; and Nick Couldry, "Theorising Media as Practice," *Social Semiotics*, vol. 14, no. 2 (2004), pp. 115-32.
36   Nick Couldry, "Media as Practice," in Nick Couldry, *Media, Society, World: Social Theory and Digital Media Practice.* London: Wiley & Sons, 2012, pp. 33-58, here p. 35.
37   Woolgar, "Configuring the User."
38   Roger Silverstone and Leslie Haddon, "Design and the Domestication of Information and Communication Technologies: Technical Change and Everyday Life," in Robin Mansell and Roger Silverstone (eds), *Communication by Design: The Politics of Information and Communication Technologies.* Oxford: Oxford University Press, 1996, pp. 44-74.

located at the time in South Africa, to perform the same search. The result was identical, and Johanna kept searching. A search query for "black hand" primarily returned pictograms or illustrations of black hands; another query for "African hand" returned images of a white person's hands holding or stretching toward a Black person's hands with overtly racist or colonial representation codes.

At that time, the theme of the racial bias of algorithms was still a subject largely overlooked by the public or researchers. Today, there is an increasing understanding about the pervasiveness and complexity of the problem with the algorithmic shaping of bodily politics—one that has led some to call Google's search algorithms "algorithms of oppression"[39] that cause ethical harm—and need for the development of an ethics of algorithms.[40] Rather than just leaving the problem after discovering it, Burai decided to try to change the results of Google's image search algorithm and introduce greater racial diversity by launching a project which she called the *World White Web*. She describes her intervention as experimental, stemming from the position of a layperson without much understanding of the technical workings of algorithms.[41] At the core of her project was the idea that—since Google's search results are generated on the basis of a ranking criteria assigned through the PageRank algorithm—the inclusion of certain alternative images of hands could be realized by generating a high enough PageRank through a media campaign. Burai took six photos of non-white hands of friends (see figs 1–6).[42]

She consulted a few individuals who work on search engine optimization to develop an understanding of how to get her pictures to the top of the search results. Along with being told that it is nearly impossible to affect Google in this way, she learned that the images needed to be uploaded and shared (without changes in the file names) by many websites with a top PageRank in Google's system. PageRank is one of the algorithms that has gained the greatest "fame" in scholarly discourse.[43] While its workings have been increasingly veiled

39   Noble, *Algorithms of Oppression*.
40   Sandvig, Hamilton, Karahalios, et al., "When the Algorithm Itself is a Racist."
41   Johanna Burai, *World White Web*, see, worldwhiteweb.net.
42   All photographs by Johanna Burai reproduced here from her project *World White Web*, ibid.
43   Beer, "The Social Power of Algorithms."

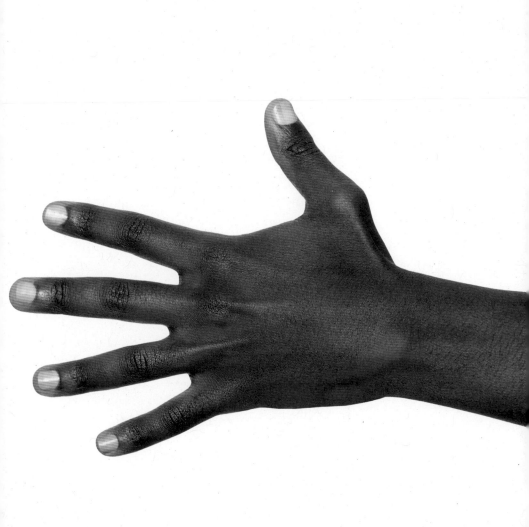

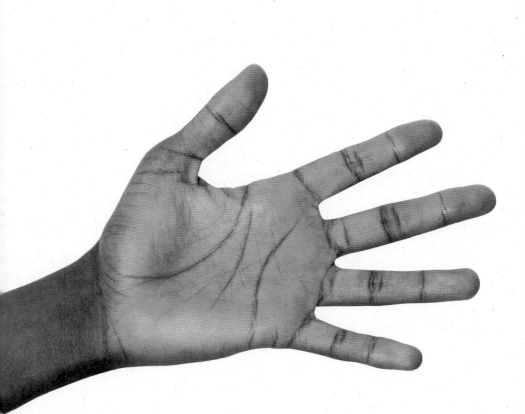

Johanna Burai, *World White Web*, 2015

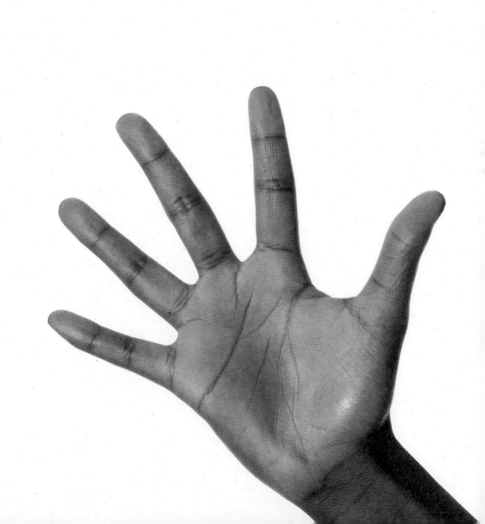

Johanna Burai, *World White Web*, 2015

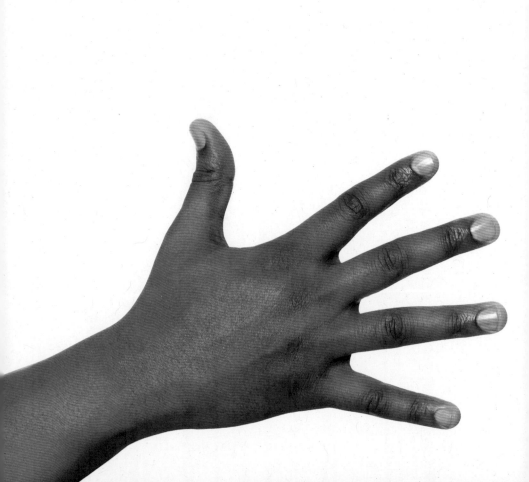

Johanna Burai, *World White Web*, 2015

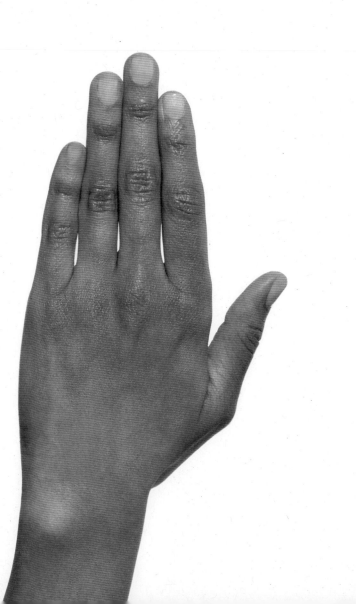

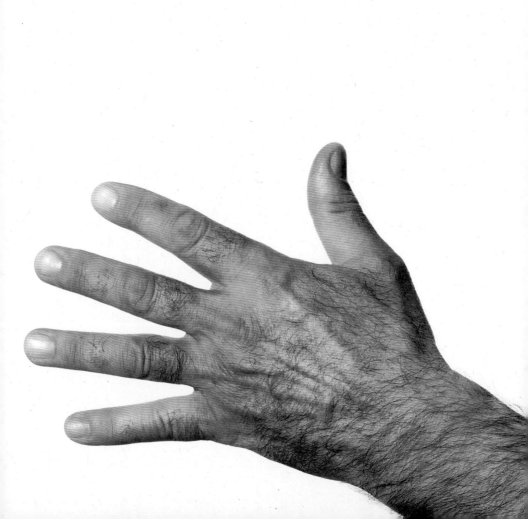

and opaque, it is considered to be among the most important sources of visibility on the Web, which works based "on a cultural assumption about relevance and importance that, to a large extent, relies on the amount of incoming links by other websites and their perceived authority."[44] Burai learned that large international news outlets like *The Guardian* or the BBC have the highest PageRank and are considered of high importance by Google's search algorithm, while local news media are less important.

In May 2015, Burai launched a campaign with the aim to get her six images uploaded and shared by as many top-ranked websites as possible. She deliberately bought a ".net" top-level domain name instead of a national one for the website; she produced a press release in which she described the problem with Google's discriminatory search results; and she asked a few friends to share information about her project through Twitter and Facebook. The attention that the project received was striking. The online popular culture newspaper *Dazed* swiftly published an article about the project but also uploaded and shared Johanna's six photos of non-white hands.[45] The BBC's music community website *Fader*, as well as *BuzzFeed*, followed suit.[46] Al Jazeera produced a thirty-minute piece on the topic of racial biases in technology. The Swedish national public broadcaster and public service radio interviewed Burai and spread her images further. In a matter of months, thanks to the significant media attention, several of her images climbed to the top results in Google's image search, where some of them remain. Burai admits that since the campaign's launch the images change position—which of her six images makes it to the top varies—but some are usually among the top-ten results. The unusual success of her intervention led her to assert at a lecture for students at a Swedish university, "Together, we can change Google."

---

44   Bucher, "Want to be on the Top?," p. 1167.
45   Frida Meinking, "World White Web is Out to Make the Internet a Bit Less White," *Dazed*, 22 May 2015, http://www.dazeddigital.comartsand culture/article/24828/1/world-white-web-is-out-to-make-the-internet -a-bit-less-white, accessed November 6, 2020.
46   Oriana Storey, "How a Designer Took on Google Over the 'World White Web,'" BBC *Newsbeat*, 14 April 2016, http://www.bbc.co.uk/newsbeat /article/36044177/how-a-designer-took-on-google-over-theworld -white-web#.tikw6ox5VN, accessed November 6, 2020.

Burai directed her intervention at only one specific search query, leaving unchanged the racial or sexual biases that other keyword searches may trigger. Yet, her case is not unique. In 2018, artist Gretchen Andrew launched her online artistic project that set out to push her paintings of the effects of ovarian cancer on patients and their suffering to the top of Google's image search results. The aim of Andrew's "Searching for Different Truths" was to provide variation from a predominantly clinical representation of searches of "ovarian cancer." Likewise, she intervened in Google's image search results of representations of specific geographic and artistic spaces, making Google's search engine into an exhibition gallery of her own art projects. The artist noted, "Definitions are highly manipulatable if you know how to structure information."[47] Richard Rogers also points to an even greater variety of artistic projects, which, in different ways, have engaged with manipulating or expressing criticism of Google's search engine results, including those of its image search function.[48] What projects such as Burai's and Andrew's tell us is that even though power might run through algorithms, resistance to the governing power of algorithms, and in particular to the politics of attention that they conduct, takes place from within the logic of the algorithm. Although starting from the premises of the algorithm, both Burai and Andrew subvert the rationalities embedded within the algorithm and hence constitute "technical politics" in Andrew Feenberg's sense.[49] Their version of technical politics—namely what we call media practices of repair—should be considered alongside hacking, technological disruption, and obfuscation, which have been identified as carrying the potential to redefine the meanings and values of technologies.

---

47   Gretchen Andrew, "Search Engine Art: Internet Imperialism and the Image in Context," paper presented at Electronic Visualisation and the Arts (EVA), in *Proceedings of Eva, London, 9–13 July* 2018. London: BCS Learning and Development, 2018, https://www.scienceopen.com /document_file/a37c0d93-f5c2-4ecc-b3ee-d795255e0222/Science Open/092_Andrew.pdf.
48   Richard Rogers, "Aestheticizing Google Critique: A 20-Year Retrospective," *Big Data & Society*, vol. 5, no. 1 (2018), n. p.
49   Feenberg, *Transforming Technology*.

User Tactics and Repair Politics

In his seminal work *Weapons of the Weak*, James Scott argues for the need to rethink dominant conceptions of resistance that take place within systems of hegemony and domination. He stresses that resistance is often thought of in terms of organized collective action with substantial, revolutionary consequences that negate the foundation of domination itself. However, more often than not, resistance is cautious and remains within the limits of what he terms "calculated conformity."[50] It is incidental, unorganized, unsystematic and individual, opportunistic and self-indulgent, with no revolutionary consequences. While such forms of resistance "imply, in their intention or meaning, an accommodation with the system of domination,"[51] and thus do not pose a fundamental challenge to the dominant power source of inequality, they represent a constant process of testing its limits and contesting power relations. Scott wrote about resistance in the context of a peasant's everyday class struggle in a village in Malaysia—a context which in many ways is very different from the relation between algorithms and uses. Nevertheless, his presentation of complicit forms of resistance is useful for an understanding of the possibilities of user agency to object to the power of algorithms.

The extent to which search algorithms such as Google's image search have been institutionalized in everyday media makes conventional forms of resistance very difficult, if not impossible. Burai's intervention was not revolutionary—it was an example of an incidental and, to a large extent, spontaneously organized media campaign with no dramatic consequences—but it tested the limits of dominant meanings produced by Google's image search results and represented a small act of power negotiation in relation to algorithmically produced racial biases. Burai's project was complicit with the logic of the algorithm, and yet it used the technology to produce an outcome that was different and unintended, at least in terms of the system. Michel de Certeau notes how in everyday contexts of oppression and dominance procedures of consumption maintain their difference "in the very space that the occupier [is] organizing."[52] Within

50   James Scott, *Weapons of the Weak: Everyday Forms of Peasant Resistance.* New Haven, CT: Yale University Press, 1985, p. 241.
51   Ibid., p. 292.
52   de Certeau, *The Practice of Everyday Life*, p. 32.

this space, difference is established through plurality and creativity enacted through tactics. For de Certeau, tactics are calculated actions "determined by the absence of a proper locus,"[53] that take place within existing structures. They are maneuvers "within the enemy's field of vision,"[54] operating "in isolated actions, blow by blow," taking advantage of "opportunities" and depending on them, "being without any base where it could stockpile its winnings, build up its own position, and plan raids." As de Certeau continues:

It must vigilantly make use of the cracks that particular conjunctions open in the surveillance of the proprietary powers. It poaches in them. It creates surprises in them. It can be where it is least expected. It is a guileful ruse.[55]

Burai's intervention was tactical, incidental, and sporadic. Her production of alternate results for a hand would most likely not last in the long run. Yet, it represented an alternative use, a tactical intervention that created a small difference, "blow by blow," within the biased politics of attention exercised by Google's image search algorithm. As such, it represents a tactical application of a politics of "repair." Repair here should not be understood literally as an intervention on malfunctioning technical code or "broken" design.[56] Burai did not repair or alter the code of the algorithm in any way. Thus, we understand repair politics as a corrective endeavor that works through improvisations, patches and ingenuity, together with and within algorithmic systems, to make them generate unintended, alternative outputs to respond to the "brokenness" or biased representational politics of algorithms. Tactical repair politics concerns agency that takes place in "an aftermath"[57] and provides a means to induce small corrections with and from within the system.

We are not suggesting, of course, that it is the responsibility of users alone to try to change and act upon power asymmetries

53   Ibid., p. 37.
54   Ibid.
55   Ibid.
56   Stephen Graham and Nigel Thrift, "Out of Order: Understanding Repair and Maintenance," *Theory, Culture & Society*, vol. 24, no. 3 (2007), pp. 1–25; and Stephen J. Jackson, "Rethinking Repair," in Gillespie, Boczkowski, and Foot (eds), *Media Technologies: Essays on Communication, Materiality, and Society*, pp. 221–40, here p. 223.
57   Ibid.

produced by algorithmic systems. Yet, the complexity of the system makes the user an equally important figure in discovering and intervening in the politics of algorithms (including, for example, those embedded in search engine results). This makes users not only part of the process of the creation of large datasets on which algorithms operate and perform their power, but also enables them tactically to work with algorithmic interfaces. Users are able to influence algorithmic processing to be conductive to specific politics, such as repair politics, which are part of a broader struggle for gender equality and balanced representation, as in the case of Burai.

Resisting
Algorithmic Power

Algorithmic power may be ontological, but it is also a media power. Many have argued that algorithmic systems resemble aspects of media institutions because algorithms such as Google's search engine increasingly behave like political and cultural institutions that operate with the politics of attention.[58] Hence, it should not be a surprise to find that questions about the politics of media representation are becoming an issue for algorithmic systems, too, and in this way an object of contestation by activists like Johanna Burai. Yet, unlike traditional forms of resistance, which in the past have resorted to "alternative" media where suppressed voices might find an arena for expression, cases like the *World White Web* project show that algorithmic resistance evolves in conjunction with the properties and logics of technologies that channel media power.[59] It is a complicit form of resistance, one that does not deny the power of algorithms but operates within their framework, using them for different ends. Such resistance necessarily has to evolve and adapt, as the algorithms eventually evolve and are adapted by their designers, too. The ontogenetic and evolving nature of algorithms pushes resistance into what Steve Jackson—writing about the work of repair—calls "an aftermath" or "the margins, breakpoints, and interstices of complex sociotechnical

---

58   Gillespie, "Algorithmically Recognizable"; Napoli, "Automated Media"; and Noble, *Algorithms of Oppression*.
59   Raymond Williams, *Television: Technology and Cultural Form*. London and New York: Routledge, 1974.

systems as they creak, flex, and bend their way through time."[60] The aftermath of algorithmic curation forces resistance to be articulated through the "repair" politics of acting upon the cultural politics of attention generated after datasets have been aggregated, computed, and curated. The notion of "repair" is a metaphor that signifies the symbolic act of correction of a perceived "brokenness" of an algorithmic system, through which the dominant meaning of algorithmic systems may also be challenged. As Burai's case shows, Google Images can simultaneously be a tool for searching the Web and a tool for political activism against the very politics of Web searches. While the actual, measurable result of such politics might seem quite insignificant (such as changing one set of results for one query), the large media attention upon which such forms of resistance depend makes it paradoxically into a strong intervention in the politics of algorithmic attention as such—by both attracting media attention to problems such as algorithmic biases and making small corrections in the search output precisely thanks to this attention.

Our analysis also points to important interlinkages between seemingly new and cutting-edge technologies with more traditional media institutions. In Burai's intervention, as in similar cases,[61] practices of traditional media campaigning were central for the reshaping of the datasets on which the Google algorithm crafts its output. Hence, we can note that while in the age of "participatory media" activists were searching for "alternative" media outlets to amplify marginal voices, in the age of algorithmic governance resistance might be increasingly dependent on collaboration with traditional media. Burai's case emphasizes the continuous crucial societal role that traditional media outlets such as the press and television play in shaping and influencing the politics of attention, including those regulated by algorithms. Traditional media outlets can serve as platforms to empower activist projects through scaling up the production of certain types of data that ultimately alter the content generated for users on the Web.[62] Instead of blaming search engines for competing with news and editorial content, traditional media must compete with

60   Jackson, "Rethinking Repair," p. 223.
61   Gillespie, "Algorithmically Recognizable."
62   Daniel Neyland, "On Organizing Algorithms," *Theory, Culture & Society*, vol. 32, no. 1 (2015), pp. 119-32.

algorithms for attention and become more aware of its own strategic role in "repairing" biases of algorithmic curation.

Of course, we must admit that traditional media and political projects like Burai's might also "break down" algorithmic curation toward progressive political change. To the extent that the politics of attention are cultural politics, they can be embraced toward multiple ends, including the strengthening of already existing biases or the amplification of violence and extremism. It is yet to be seen how such potentially harmful uses of technologies and "repair politics" might play out, particularly in light of the mechanisms with which platforms aim to police harmful online content.[63]

We conclude with two suggestions for theoretical possibilities and future studies. First, more empirical and theoretical research is needed for strengthening the understanding of the role of traditional media outlets and campaigning in shaping the output of algorithms. Second, we should be attentive to the ways in which users engage with algorithmic systems across contexts, and further explore the media practices and politics through which political agency works with and through algorithms, reshapes their output, and attempts to redefine their social meaning. Technology is not a thing but "an ambivalent process of development suspended between different possibilities,"[64] always in the making, remaking, and unmaking. The engagement with technology as always in the making would also include a mapping of different forms of resistance toward the intended usage of technologies.

Resistance being an intrinsic part of the shaping of technologies demands more attention, especially in the context of algorithmic culture. We have traced a very specific form of algorithmic resistance that emerges from within the system, a tactic that is reformist rather than revolutionary.[65] Many other ways of resisting algorithmic power—and in that way shaping algorithmic culture—are thinkable (e.g. more structural approaches advocating for regulation at the policy level or individual tactics of obfuscation). In all of these possible cases, it will be crucial to continue to recognize the co-constructed nature of algorithms and to keep locating user agency and resistance in relation to them as they, their uses, and resistance co-evolve.

63   Gillespie, "Algorithmically Recognizable."
64   Feenberg, *Transforming Technology*, p. 15.
65   de Certeau, *The Practice of Everyday Life*.

We wish to thank the anonymous reviewers, and Jesse Haapoja for their comments and suggestions. Special thanks to Johanna Burai for sharing and discussing her project with us. We also would like to thank Taylor & Francis Ltd (www.tandfonline.com) for permission to adapt and print our article originally published in *Information, Communication & Society* in August 2019. https://doi.org/10.1080/1369118X.2019.1657162

ping-ponged

aftermath

+   Daniel Neugebauer is head of the Department of Communications and Cultural Education at Haus der Kulturen der Welt. Educated as a literary scholar, he is interested in the interfaces of communication and educational work. Having trained at the Kunsthalle Bielefeld, from 2012 to 2018 he headed the division of marketing, mediation, and fundraising at the Van Abbemuseum in the Netherlands. In 2016 / 17 he coordinated marketing for documenta 14 in Kassel and Athens. In recent years, inclusion and queering have been the focus of his institutional practice.

+ **Alyk Blue** is an interdisciplinary artist, writer, and melancholic fantasist. They try to find meaning in the mundane and make the mundane tolerable. You can find a portion of their current work on Instagram @alykblue.

+ **Johanna Burai** is an art director and multidisciplinary designer based between Stockholm and London. She mainly works in the cultural field of art, music and fashion, creating ideas and concepts for commercial and self-initiated projects. Her project World White Web (2015) brings attention to the norm of whiteness in search engines as an example of the systematic racism experienced by people of color in everyday life.

+ **Luce deLire** is a ship with eight sails and she lays off the quay. A time traveler and collector of mediocre jokes by day, when night falls, she turns into a philosopher, performer, and media theorist. She could be seen curating, performing, directing, planning, publishing, and (most naturally) philosophizing at and on various topics and events. She is working on and with treason, post secularism, self-destruction, fascism, seduction, and Spinoza's metaphysics of infinity—all in mixed media. www.getaphilosopher.com

+ **Anne Kaun** is an associate professor in Media and Communication Studies at Södertörn University, Sweden. Her research interests include media theory, mediated temporalities, algorithmic culture, as well as automation and artificial intelligence from a humanistic social science perspective. Her works have appeared in, among others, *New Media & Society*; *Media, Culture & Society; International Journal of Communication*; as well as the *European Journal of Cultural Studies*. Her book *Crisis and Critique: A Brief History of Media Participation in Times of Crisis* was published by Zed Books in 2016.

+   Rhea Ramjohn is a poet, educator, and podcaster from Trinidad and Tobago via Boston and Berlin. She is the host of the science podcast *Hormonal* as well as executive producer of *Tanti Table*. Her work centers vernacular expression and social justice, which is most evident in her work as co-founder of Black Brown Berlin and her poetry film *Live chile!*, commissioned in 2020 by the Haus der Kulturen der Welt.

+   Calah P Toussaint-Amat (Amat Toussaint Visuals) created the illustrations of the hands for Rhea Ramjohn's contribution. On Instagram she can be found at @amat_toussaint.

+   Julia Velkova is an assistant professor/research fellow in Technology and Social Change at the Department for Thematic Studies, Linköping University, Sweden. She is also a research affiliate at the Global Media Technologies and Cultures Lab led by Lisa Parks at the University of California, Santa Barbara. She is currently involved in several projects that explore questions of labor, temporality, and politics of difference in converging digital- and energy infrastructures, with specific focus on data centers in the Nordic countries. Her research has been published in journals such as *New Media & Society*; *Culture Machine*; *Big Data & Society*; and the *International Journal of Cultural Studies*, among others.

Colophon

Das Neue Alphabet (The New Alphabet) is a publication series
by HKW (Haus der Kulturen der Welt).

The series is part of the HKW project *Das Neue Alphabet*
(2019–2022), supported by the Federal Government
Commissioner for Culture and the Media due to a ruling
of the German Bundestag.

Series Editors: Detlef Diederichsen, Anselm Franke,
      Katrin Klingan, Daniel Neugebauer, Bernd Scherer
Project Management: Philipp Albers
Managing Editor: Martin Hager
Copy-Editing: Mandi Gomez, Hannah Sarid de Mowbray
Design Concept: Olaf Nicolai with Malin Gewinner,
      Hannes Drißner

Vol. 5: *Skin and Code*
Editor: Daniel Neugebauer
Coordination: Laida Hadel
Contributors: Alyk Blue, Johanna Burai, Luce deLire, i-PÄD,
      Anne Kaun, Rhea Ramjohn, Calah P Toussaint-Amat,
      Julia Velkova
Translations: Kevin Kennedy, Jacqueline Todd
Graphic Design: Malin Gewinner, Hannes Drißner,
      Markus Dreßen
Type-Setting: Hannah Witte
Fonts: FK Raster (Florian Karsten), Suisse BP Int'l (Ian Party),
      Lyon Text (Kai Bernau)
Image Editing: Scancolor Reprostudio GmbH, Leipzig
Printing and Binding: Gutenberg Beuys Feindruckerei GmbH,
      Langenhagen

Published by:
Spector Books
Harkortstr. 10
01407 Leipzig
www.spectorbooks.com

Distribution:

Germany, Austria: GVA Gemeinsame Verlagsauslieferung
        Göttingen GmbH & Co. KG, www.gva-verlage.de
Switzerland: AVA Verlagsauslieferung AG, www.ava.ch
France, Belgium: Interart Paris, www.interart.fr
UK: Central Books Ltd, www.centralbooks.com
USA, Canada, Central and South America, Africa:
        ARTBOOK | D.A.P. www.artbook.com
Japan: twelvebooks, www.twelve-books.com
South Korea: The Book Society, www.thebooksociety.org
Australia, New Zealand: Perimeter Distribution,
        www.perimeterdistribution.com

Haus der Kulturen der Welt
John-Foster-Dulles-Allee 10
D-10557 Berlin
www.hkw.de

Haus der Kulturen der Welt is a business division of Kultur-
veranstaltungen des Bundes in Berlin GmbH (KBB).

Director: Bernd Scherer
Managing Director: Charlotte Sieben
Chairwoman of the Supervisory Board: Federal
        Government Commissioner for Culture and the Media
        Prof. Monika Grütters MdB

Haus der Kulturen der Welt is supported by

Minister of State
for Culture and the Media   Federal Foreign Office

First Edition
Printed in Germany
ISBN: 978-3-95905-461-4

Recently published:
Vol. 1: *The New Alphabet*
Vol. 2: *Listen to Lists*
Vol. 3: *Counter_Readings of the Body*
Vol. 4: *Echo*
Vol. 5: *Skin and Code*

Forthcoming:
Vol. 6: *Carrier Bag Fiction* (April 2021)
Vol. 7: *Making* (May 2021)

Vol. 6:	*Carrier Bag Fiction*
Editors:	Sarah Shin, Mathias Zeiske
Contrib.:	Federico Campagna, Dorothee Elmiger, Ursula K. Le Guin, Enis Maci, Leanne Betasamosake Simpson, Anna Lowenhaupt Tsing , a. o.
ISBN:	978–3–95905–463–8
	April 2021

What if humanity's primary inventions were not the Hero's spear but rather a basket of wild oats, a medicine bundle, a story. Ursula K. Le Guin's 1986 essay *The Carrier Bag Theory of Fiction* presents a feminist story of technology that centres on the collective sustenance of life, and reimagines the carrier bag as a tool for telling strangely realistic fictions. New writings and images respond to Le Guin's narrative practice of world-making through gathering and holding.

Vol. 7:	*Making*
Editors:	Nick Houde, Katrin Klingan, Johanna Schindler
Contrib.:	Luis Campos, Maria Chehonadskih, Reece Cox, Ana Guzmán, Hao Liang, Hu Fang, Elisabeth Povinelli, Kaushik Sunder Rajan, Sophia Roosth
ISBN	978–3–95905–465–2
	May 2021

Who produces what, and how? What tools and technologies, what values and intentions are fed into the process? What part do power and control play in the context of semi-autonomous technologies that will shape our future world? The book's essays and artist contributions focus on the practices and politics of production as a response to our contemporary processes of planetary transformation.